W9-BQX-084

SPIRITUAL WARFARE

SPIRITUAL WARFARE

Victory over the Powers of This Dark World

Timothy M. Warner

CROSSWAY BOOKS • WHEATON, ILLINOIS
A DIVISION OF GOOD NEWS PUBLISHERS

Spiritual Warfare.

Copyright © 1991 by Timothy M. Warner.

Published by Crossway Books, a division of
Good News Publishers, Wheaton, Illinois 60187.

All rights reserved. No part of this publication may be reproduced, stored
in a retrieval system or transmitted in any form by any means, electronic,
mechanical, photocopy, recording or otherwise, without the prior permission of the publisher, except as provided by USA copyright law.

Cover design/illustration: Dennis Hill

First printing, 1991

Printed in the United States of America

Unless otherwise noted, all Bible quotations are taken from *Holy Bible:
New International Version*, copyright © 1978 by the New York
International Bible Society. Used by permission of Zondervan Bible
Publishers.

ISBN 0-89107-607-7

T A B L E   O F

CONTENTS

INTRODUCTION

THIS BOOK HAD ITS genesis as the Church Growth Lectures at Fuller Theological Seminary in October 1988. I am very grateful to the faculty of the School of World Mission at Fuller for the invitation which prompted me to put these thoughts into written form.

The original lectures have been revised and put into shorter chapters. More illustrations have been added and even a few new ideas expressed. I find my thinking constantly expanding as I continue to study this subject and to minister in this area of human need. I am reluctant to be called an expert on this topic, but I gladly add the ideas expressed here to the wide-ranging discussion of this critical issue today.

I am grateful to many who have encouraged me to write and to Crossway Books for their competent assistance in seeing the manuscript into book form. I trust that God will use it to help equip the Church with complete confidence in the final victory of our Lord over our enemy and in our our sufficiency in Him to see the Great Commission carried to completion.

CHAPTER ONE

THE GLORY OF GOD

Some Current Perspectives on the Conflict

There can be little doubt that we are living in an age of more overt demonic activity in our American society than has ever been seen here. It is not that Satan and demons have been inactive in our early history. They tailor their tactics to the historic setting, and covert activity served their purposes better in our earlier history. They still operate under cover most of the time, but for a variety of reasons they are much more in evidence in our society today than at other times in American history. This has tended to make Western Christians much more aware of what is called spiritual warfare than ever before.

This theme has always been present in Scripture, but our faulty belief systems have caused us to ignore what others see as obvious. Missionaries are more apt to treat demons as real beings than those who know only Western culture, but even missionaries react with surprise when they finally understand how "Western" their view of the Bible has been. The following missionary report may be a bit more extreme than some, but many have had similar experiences.

His eyes were glassy, his clothes ragged, his hair mat-
ted, and he was desperate. "I'm going to kill this animal," he repeated three times. I thought he was
talking about me. The lady of the house gave us all
some strong coffee, but he didn't want it. Suddenly
he fell on the floor, knocking the dishes off the table.
As we dragged him out of the house, he looked up at
me and said, "Have mercy on me." Then I recognized
his problem. He was demon possessed. These spells
began after he stopped attending an evangelical
church and turned to spiritism.

I remembered the words of Jesus. "Behold, I give
you [authority] over all the power of the enemy, and
nothing by any means shall hurt you." I felt I should
rebuke the demon in the name of Jesus, but what if
nothing happened? All the people gathered would
ridicule me. . . .

There I was—a defeated missionary in the interior
of Brazil, ready to pack up and go home. When face
to face with the enemy, I was afraid.[1]

Many missionaries have a story they could tell
about an encounter with demonic power. But they usually don't tell it because it didn't end with victory, or
because they are afraid their listeners will not have a
background against which to understand it. It is generally agreed that we are in a spiritual battle in the
Christian life, and especially so when we serve in fron-
tier mission situations. Unfortunately very few, even
among missionary recruits, have received any training
(either theoretical or practical) in dealing with demons
and demonic power.

I grew up in a Christian home, attended an evangelical college where I majored in Bible, spent three years
at a theological seminary which specialized in inductive
Bible study, and then taught for two years in the Bible

college before going to West Africa to be a missionary. I was stationed in a tribal village to do evangelism and church planting, having received no orientation to cross-cultural ministry either in seminary or in a missionary candidate school prior to departure or from fellow missionaries after my arrival on the field. Missions courses were very few in those days, and the two I remember had almost nothing to do with actual missionary service, least of all with dealing with demons. I am appalled at what I did not know, on the one hand, about culture in general and animistic thought systems in particular and, on the other hand, about the Christian position on confronting demonic power.

Until very recently there has been a lack of reliable books available on the subject of the spiritual encounter in which we are all engaged and even fewer which relate specifically to a missionary or evangelistic context. This is one of the reasons for the lack of training available on this subject. As Alan R. Tippett pointed out in an article back in 1960, we tend to teach courses in areas in which good textbooks are available.[2] The emergence of reliable literature on spiritual warfare helps to explain the spread of college and seminary courses dealing with this subject in some fashion.

The fact is, however, that neither God nor Satan has changed since the first encounter in the Garden of Eden. Spiritual conflict has been a part of human experience from that time on. Genesis 3:15 provides a key element in establishing the context in which all the rest of the Bible must be viewed: "And I will put enmity between you and the woman, and between your offspring and hers; he will crush your head, and you will strike his heel." Spiritual conflict permeates the Biblical record from that time on, and today we are involved in this conflict whether we want to be or not. We have tried to ignore the enemy, but that only gives him a strategic advantage in the ongoing battle.

Let it be stated clearly at the beginning of this study, however, that the outcome of the war is not in doubt. God's sovereign power is in no danger whatever. Through the Cross and the Resurrection the Lord Jesus Christ decisively defeated our enemy. For His own good and sufficient reasons, however, God has not yet executed the final judgment against the enemy. But it is time that we take our enemy seriously because of the high stakes for which this war is being fought. Spiritual warfare is often misunderstood because it is assumed that demonic activity in our lives only begins with overt activity which can clearly be assigned to demons. The truth is, however, that the battle begins the minute we are born. Satan has a consuming desire to control the destiny of every person on Planet Earth. He is the one who blinds the minds of unbelievers, "so that they cannot see the light of the gospel of the glory of Christ, who is the image of God" (2 Corinthians 4:4).

The battle takes on special significance when a person turns from the realm of Satan's control and begins life under the Lordship of Jesus Christ. The essence of the conflict before conversion is a matter of the truth about salvation. After conversion it is still a matter of truth, but now the focus changes to the truth about God and the truth about ourselves.

Satan's primary tactic is deception or clever lying, and the degree to which we believe any of his lies and come under the influence of deception is the degree to which Satan or demons have control of our lives.

The arguments about whether a demon can be in the body of a Christian and whether a believer can be "possessed" by a demon often serve to divert our attention from the more fundamental issue of deception in these basic areas of belief about God and about ourselves in relation to God. Not to recognize this "truth encounter," as Neil Anderson calls it,[3] is to continue in bondage to the deception which is guiding one's life.

As I am writing this I am working with a lady who has just discovered that she has two levels of belief. One is an essentially intellectual level. At that level she can enunciate correct Christian doctrine. But there is also a functional level of belief which is actually quite different from the one she verbalizes. At this level she is really very angry at God and her view of herself is almost totally negative.

We will come back to this theme later, but for now it serves to raise many questions—questions like: How do we know demons are involved in this deception? How do we know it isn't just the operation of the flesh? Aren't we ascribing more activity to Satan than is warranted by the Scriptures?

With those questions in mind, it may be helpful to review briefly how this spiritual conflict started.

The Roots of the Conflict

Satan's Jealousy of God

The roots of this conflict are found in an event which took place in Heaven or in the heavenly realms and which involved God and one of the highest angels. The Bible does not give us in narrative form the events which led to the fall of Satan from his original angelic identity and function to the identity and function in which we encounter him today. We are, however, given a clear portrayal of his utterly evil nature and work based on his extreme jealousy of and hatred for God.

There is general agreement among evangelical writers on this subject that Satan was probably one of the highest-ranking angels in the angelic hierarchy. There is some Biblical evidence to indicate that he may have been a cherub—one of those majestic beings pictured as the guardians of the throne of God (Ezekiel 28:16; Exodus 25:19; Psalm 18:10; Hebrews 9:5). In the Old Testament it was cherubs who figuratively stood guard at each end of the mercy seat where God dwelt in the midst of His people. Recognizing the caution that must be used when projecting earthly figures into the heavenly realm, it would seem fair to say that in his original state Satan perceived the glory of God from a perspective shared by few other created beings.

How he could have abdicated that position is beyond our comprehension, but I suggest one possible scenario which grows out of implications of Scriptural teaching, if not from direct statement. We are not told when angels were created, but it must have been prior to the creation of our world because when the foundations of the earth were laid, "the morning stars sang together and all the angels shouted for joy" (Job 38:7). Yet, I am inclined to believe that the creation of angels was done in connection with our creation and not at some indefinite time in eternity past because of Paul's statement in Colossians 1:16 listing them with other elements in the creation of the world and because of their close connection with many things related to the world down to and including the climax of human history.

Lucifer was apparently assigned along with the other cherubim to guard the glory of God. God obviously does not need "guards" because of any inherent weakness in Himself. But in His infinite foreknowledge, He knew that some of the creatures who would come from His hand would become alienated from Him, even becoming His enemies. Satan would challenge God over the issue of glory in the realm of God's human creatures. Others of His creatures would therefore need to be reflectors of His glory and, in some sense, guardians of it among the population of Planet Earth. Assuming that

Lucifer began his existence as a "guardian cherub" (Ezekiel 28:14) in the heavenly realms, he knew the glory of God as few others of God's creatures knew it.

At some point in the creative process, Lucifer allowed jealousy of God and His glory to possess him until he had an insatiable desire to be like God, if not actually to take God's place. We see this surface in his attempt to get Jesus to worship him in the temptation in the wilderness (Matthew 4:9), in his manifestation in the man of sin who in a future day "opposes and exalts himself over everything that is called God or is worshiped" and "sets himself up in God's temple, proclaiming himself to be God" (2 Thessalonians 2:4), and again in the activity of the beast in Revelation 13.

I am aware of the problems raised in applying Isaiah 14 to Satan, but I believe that a metaphorical hermeneutic is called for in dealing with the oracles on the nations in Isaiah. At key points in Scripture Babylon is a type of or figure for the world or world system, and the "prince" or "king" of that world system is Satan.

Even if the reference in Isaiah 14 is limited to the human king of Babylon, he represents a man so controlled by Satan that he speaks the words of Satan. Geoffrey Grogan's comment on the text is pertinent:

> This passage itself seems to be echoed by the Lord Jesus in Luke 10:18 where language applied here to the king of Babylon is used of Satan. Nothing could be more appropriate, for the pride of the king of Babylon was truly Satanic. When Satan works his malign will through rulers of this world, he reproduces his own wicked qualities in them, so that they become virtual shadows of which he is the substance.[4]

I, therefore, see this passage as a window through which to view Satan.

In the passage we find a series of statements revealing the fatal line of thinking which led to Lucifer's fall. First, this created being expresses dissatisfaction with his created order as an angel and aspires to enter the realm of being reserved exclusively for God ("I will ascend to heaven," v. 13a). Second, he voices unholy ambition to be over his peers, the other angels ("I will raise my throne above the stars of God," v. 13b). Third, assuming the "mount of assembly" to refer to the throne of Messiah, we see Satan challenging Christ for His position of kingly authority—a challenge he carried out unsuccessfully in the wilderness temptation ("I will sit enthroned on the mount of assembly," v. 13c). Fourth, given the association of clouds with the glory of God in the Old Testament (e.g., Exodus 13:21; 40:34-38), he seeks the position of glory occupied by God ("I will ascend above the tops of the clouds," v. 14a). And finally, he betrays his ultimate objective—to be a God like Yahweh and thus to challenge his position of sovereignty ("I will make myself like the Most High," v. 14b).

However, a created being cannot rise to a level higher than that for which he was created by God. So rather than starting a process of glorification by his rebellion against God, Satan began a process of degradation. As Chafer says in his theology of Satan, the world of evil and suffering which is Satan's domain today is more likely the evidence "of his failure rather than the realization of his purpose."[5] Or, to quote Grogan again, "It is a strange paradox that nothing makes a being less like God than the urge to be his equal."[6] Therefore, rather than becoming glorious like God, Lucifer became the epitome of that which is ungodly.

Satan's Jealousy of God's Children

But there may be another element in Satan's fall which will help us to understand the conflict in which we are involved today. It may be that the fall of Satan did not occur until after the creation of man. As we have noted, the angels were certainly created before human beings. It may be, however, that, when Lucifer saw this new order of beings created "in the image of God" (Genesis 1:26, 27), his jealousy was intensified. While these new persons were created lower than the angels for their time on earth, they were also created with the potential for glorification. Being "in the image of God," they had the capacity for likeness to God which Lucifer as an angel did not possess. Indeed, it is clear from passages such as Romans 8:17, 30, and 9:23 that glorification is God's plan for His people. So if Lucifer was jealous of God over the issue of glory, he is also jealous of God's highest creation over the same issue.

Satan would like to make a frontal attack on God in order to claim His position of glory, but that is an impossibility. The difference between the level of Deity occupied by Yahweh and the level of angels occupied by Satan was and is so vast that Satan's challenge was ludicrous. This may well be the idea behind the passages in the Psalms which picture God laughing at the enemies of His people (Psalm 2:4; 37:13; 59:8). The children of God, however, are vulnerable; and Satan pioneered the tactic (used by many a scoundrel from that day on) of getting at an enemy by attacking or threatening to attack that person's children. Because God's children are for their time on earth confined to material bodies in a world in which even fallen angels have some measure of supernatural power, Satan's plan became one of using his angelic power to deceive God's children, and thus to divert them from reflecting God's glory here and from achieving the potential with which God made them for glorification after death.

Satan's first desire was to have the other creatures of God worship him and give him the glory which was rightfully due only to God. That would not be an easy task to accomplish, however, especially if he made a frontal approach. His aim would have to be accomplished by trickery.

Satan's Strategy

The principal tactic of Satan in his conflict with God from the very beginning, therefore, has been to deceive God's children into believing that the tremendous potential which resides within them can be realized by living life under their own control rather than under God's control and to believe that there is a legitimate source of power other than Yahweh. There is no doubt that this human creature made in the image of God had incredible potential. The humanists who say there are vast untapped resources within us are partly right. Satan was wise enough to recognize this, and he has been trying to sell the lie of humanism (i.e., we can achieve our full potential apart from a relationship with the Creator) in one form or another ever since his first encounter with Eve in the Garden.

As we meet this kind of humanism in the New Age Movement, we find a clear example of how Satan uses his deception to lure people into accepting knowledge and power from him without acknowledging that he is the source. C. S. Lewis has a remarkably perceptive insight on this in *Screwtape Letters* when he has Screwtape write to Wormwood:

Our policy, for the moment, is to conceal ourselves. Of course this has not always been so. We are really faced with a cruel dilemma. When the humans disbelieve in our existence, we lose all the pleasing results of direct terrorism, and we make no magicians. On the other hand, when they believe in us, we cannot make them materialists and skeptics. At least, not yet. I have great hopes that we shall learn in due time how to emotionalize and mythologize their science to such an extent that what is, in effect, a belief in us (though not under that name) will creep in while the human mind remains closed to belief in the Enemy. The 'Life Force,' the worship of sex, and some aspects of Psychoanalysis may here prove useful. If once we can produce our perfect work—the Materialist Magician, the man, not using, but veritably worshiping, what he vaguely calls 'Forces' while denying the existence of 'spirits'—then the end of the war will be in sight.[7]

So, in the New Age Movement God as a sovereign Creator-Sustainer has been eliminated from one's belief system; people, individually and collectively, have become god. The "latent powers of the mind" are thought to be developed in various ways, and channeling enhances that power by putting one in touch with people from other ages. This all involves significant demonstrations of power which, no matter how the New Age devotees define it, is in truth coming from demons. In evangelizing such persons, therefore, we must be prepared for a confrontation with spiritual powers—a power encounter—and must in addition be prepared to expose Satanic deception with the truth and to demonstrate the power of God over the deceiving spirits, not simply to talk about it.

For example, a young man in a nearby community called me to ask for help in dealing with out-of-body experiences he was having. These experiences began after he became involved in a program advertised to help one develop his full potential and to achieve his aspirations in life. The leader assured them at the first meeting that the program was not a cult and was, in fact, not even religious. To prove this, the leader wrote "GOD" on the chalkboard and had each member of the class come up and erase "GOD" off the board as a symbol that they were not going to look to a God to do something for them—they were going to do it for themselves. Then they did the same thing with "JESUS CHRIST." The deeper the young man got into the teachings of the group, however, the more strange experiences he began to have. When he asked the leader of the group about these strange happenings, he was told not to worry about them—such things were common.

When the young man acknowledged that he had become the victim of deception, renounced the powers he had unknowingly invited into his life, and recommitted himself to the Lordship of Christ and the truth of Scripture, the out-of-body experiences stopped.

But there is another factor at work in the human situation which Satan capitalizes on to promote his deception. While we humans were made with tremendous potential, we were not made to be autonomous. We were made to live in human societies requiring relationships of many kinds. And as Marguerite Shuster points out so perceptively in her book *Power, Pathology, Paradox*, people need power to handle these relationships. She says:

> Utterly to lack power, to produce no effects, or to make no difference anywhere or to anyone is not to exist. To *feel* impotent is to encounter *fear* of nonexistence, fear that nothing matters, fear that everything is utterly meaningless and hopeless because one is helpless.[8]

There is a sense, then, in which power is essential for everyone—for life itself. Satan can therefore appeal to this need for power at the most fundamental level of human existence, and he uses the appeal effectively.

The need for power over circumstances, over people, and over the future has always been a human concern. We either find this power in God, or we become susceptible to the offers of power in these areas from Satan. The long history of magic, sorcery, divination, and other forms of occult practices witnesses to this. And the current popularity of the occult, and specifically of New Age teachings, is evidence that the desire for power in these areas still exists.

So, on the one hand, we have a powerful, rebellious angel who is committed to war with Yahweh over the issue of glory, and, on the other hand, we have an order of beings who were uniquely endowed with the image of God so that they might live "for the praise of his glory" (Ephesians 1:12; cf. v. 6). Satan knows that while we humans have been created in the image of God for this high purpose, we need an ongoing relationship with God to accomplish that purpose. Further, he now sees us as the avenue through which he can carry on his war against God. If he can lure us with his offers of information and power or intimidate us with his shows of strength, he can, he believes, frustrate the plan of God.

Thus Satan's jealousy of God provides powerful motivation for him in this war. Jealousy is one of the stronger emotions as far as moving to action. Allowed to develop unchecked, jealousy passes through three stages. First, we see what someone else has and we want it. At the second stage, we realize that the object of our jealousy can never be ours; so we hate the other person for having what we can't have. And finally, that hate leads us to try to deprive the other person of what he or she has, whether that be something physical or something like one's reputation. Lucifer quickly reached the third stage, and his one ambition today is to deprive God of His glory and to keep us from participating in it.

The Devil cannot deprive God of glory in Heaven, but he can keep God from having His rightful glory ascribed to Him by people on earth. He does this by keeping them blind to God's true character and to His purpose in creating and re-creating them and by keeping them ignorant of the power which is available to them to achieve that purpose. And when some of the people on earth do seek the Lord and try to walk in His ways, Satan can at least keep them from living in a manner that is "for the praise of his glory." The key in either case is to get them to live self-centered rather than God-centered lives, to buy into his lies about life, and to substitute Satan's kind of power for God's power.

CHAPTER TWO

WORLDVIEWS IN CONFLICT

FOLLOWING A CLASS I taught as a visiting professor at another school, a missionary who had come to take the class was having dinner with the college president. The president asked him what he had learned. His answer somewhat surprised his host. He said, "I changed my worldview."

Most of us probably do not have much difficulty with the theory or the theology of spiritual conflict, but we have considerable difficulty when we begin applying it. The reason for the difficulty is that we have a worldview problem. Spirits are not a functional part of our worldview. We can theologize about the spirit world with no problem; but when we attempt to bring spirits into the explanation system for the phenomena of our lives, we have major problems.

To put it plainly, spirits are not very real to us. In many, if not most, aspects of our lives we are more humanistic and materialistic than we like to admit. That is admittedly a strong accusation. To test it, just ask yourself: If you get into a discussion which degenerates into an argument, do you control your emotions better when an important person shows up whom you would like to impress, or when you are aware that the Holy Spirit is present? People are much more real to us than spirits are. Unfortunately, this applies to the Holy Spirit as well as to demonic spirits.

Worldview Defined

Worldview is the thought system we develop for explaining the world around us and our experiences in it. It is determined almost entirely by the society in which we grow up. In most instances, it is something we absorb subconsciously more than something we adopt after careful study, although study can change worldview drastically. James Sire defines this as the "set of presuppositions or assumptions which we hold (consciously or subconsciously) about the basic make-up of our world."[1] It is a set of categories we develop into which we plug the data of our experience to give it meaning.

To put it another way, it is like looking at the world through a good optical system or a bad one. One of my sisters happened to be studying at the Learning Disabilities Center at the University of California/Long Beach at a time when the director of the center was working on a new discovery. Quite by accident the director had observed that placing a sheet of colored acetate over a page of print corrected the visual problem a child was having seeing the words on the page correctly. Further research showed a clear correlation between color and visually oriented learning disabilities in many cases. Since that time my sister has had the thrill of having a person put on their tinted lenses for the first time and say, "Is that what it is supposed to look like?" whether the "it" was a map, a landscape, a page of print, or a sunset.

Worldview is a set of lenses through which we view the world. Wrong worldviews will produce faulty explanations for the experiences of life, just as a faulty optical system will produce depth perception problems or problems such as dyslexia. And just as the person with the dyslexia doesn't know what "normal" vision is, so a person with a wrong worldview does not know that a critical factor is missing from his explanation system for his world.

Stanley Mooneyham put it this way:

> In my own experience traveling overseas, I have never personally come across demon possession that I could recognize. I have, however, many times been conscious of spiritual battles, where the presence of evil was very real, and I was conscious that a spiritual conflict was taking place.
>
> I am sure that had I had a different cultural background and different "eyes" for perceiving the world, I might have seen the visible manifestations of this demonic activity. My technology-oriented, rationalistic, Western culture simply prevented me from seeing what the people of other cultures see and experience in a more tangible way.[2]

A favorite college professor of mine used to say, "People may not live what they profess, but they will always live what they believe." *Worldview is what we really believe.* The "profession" level of belief is usually a theoretical or theological statement of the accepted dogmas of one's religion. This is the level at which religion is usually studied and discussed by the scholars and at which it is taught to the followers. The followers, however, usually practice the religion at a very different level—a level that is very life-related. This is often referred to as the "folk" level of the religion. Worldview finds its expression most clearly at the folk level of our beliefs, not the intellectual level. So if you want to find out what individuals really believe—what their worldview really is—you don't ask them, you watch them. You especially observe them under pressure and in crisis. What they do at such times reveals their real belief system, especially their beliefs about God and spiritual power.

Animistic Worldviews

Most of the non-Western world and large segments of the Western world have a folk-level set of religious beliefs akin to what is generally called animism. Animism is not a world religion like Islam or Hinduism. That is, it does not have formalized belief systems based on a holy book or books, but it is very widespread and does have some common elements in most of its expressions.

One of those common elements is that everything in the world—animal, vegetable, and mineral—shares the same kind of spiritual power. Different terms are used for this power, but it is something like electricity. It is in itself neither good nor bad; it is neutral. Just as electricity may light a room or kill a person, this impersonal spiritual power may give you good luck or it may kill you.

Besides this impersonal power, there is in animism a common belief in spirit beings who are thought to be involved in all aspects of life here on Planet Earth. These spirits may be associated with natural objects, with people, or with the dead (ancestors); and they may be good or evil in nature. A person who has an animistic worldview cannot conceive of a purely scientific view of the world. In his view the physical and spiritual are inseparable.

Western Worldviews

The worldview of the typical Christian in the Western world, on the other hand, has two discrete, functional realms. One of these is the supernatural. It is where God and whatever other spirit beings there may be are located. The other is the natural realm. This is the created world, which operates according to "natural laws"—laws which God established in creation, but which today operate without any spirit involvement. This worldview causes us to ask either-or kinds of questions: Is it supernatural or is it natural? Is it religious or is it scientific? Is it spiritual or is it psychological? Is it sacred or is it secular? Is it demonic or is it just the flesh?

We assume that these two realms are clearly separated from each other and that, whatever connection there may be between them, it is not a very functional one. We accept the premise that for any phenomenon in the natural realm there is a cause in the natural realm. The cause of any observable phenomenon or of any experience here in the natural realm will seldom be from the realm of spirits. Occasionally there may be "miracles," which fall into this category, but they are rare. We have become functional deists in too many cases. We assume that we have a Christian worldview because we posit God as Creator. But we also assume that He is now on His throne up in Heaven and that the world is being run by scientific laws which have no functional spiritual components. That is deism.

Biblical Worldview

I must conclude, however, that this worldview is a part of Satan's strategy to get us to act on the basis of error rather than on the basis of truth. The Scriptures clearly teach that there are three orders of beings who are parts of our world—namely, Deity, angels, and human beings—and that these three orders are in constant, functional contact.

The Realm of God

The highest of these orders is God Himself. He is *sui generis*; He is the only occupant of the realm of Deity. Satan has tried in many ways to create the illusion that there are other "gods" besides Yahweh. One of those approaches is the dualism which in one way or another makes Satan the eternal counterpart of God. If Satan cannot achieve his original goal of being like God in His glory, he will settle for being on the same level of power as God but with a different agenda—an eternal God and an eternal Devil. The fact is, however, that God is eternal, but Satan is not. He belongs to the order of being called angels, not to the order of being called God. There is one God, the uncreated Creator.

The Realm of Angels

The second of the three realms of being is that of angels. They are a created order (Colossians 1:16), and, according to the statements of Scripture, they perform a wide variety of functions in the universe of which our world is a part. The fanciful treatment of angels during the Middle Ages caused the Reformers to back off from the subject,[3] and the Enlightenment and the rise of the industrial-technological age furthered that withdrawal. Paul Hiebert refers to this process as "the mystification of religion" and the "secularization of science."[4] The world came to be seen as having two functional realms—natural and supernatural. The realm of the supernatural came to be thought of as including God and angels and whatever other spirit beings there may be, and it became more and more "other-worldly," while the natural realm became "this worldly."[5]

In the thinking of the sophisticated Westerner, contact between the supernatural realm and the "real," natural realm became less and less. And as this worldview came to dominate our formal educational systems, most of our society, including evangelical Christians, were influenced by it. Not only was our own worldview unconsciously molded by it, but we exported it to the Two-thirds World via our missionaries to the extent that Lesslie Newbigin could correctly argue in his book *Honest Religion for Secular Man* that Christian missionaries have been one of the most secularizing forces in the world.[6]

It is not difficult to see how Satan has been uniquely successful in depriving God of the glory He deserves in this process. We missionaries taught, for example, that it isn't spirits which make crops grow or not grow; it is whether or not one practices scientific agriculture. So we got fertilizer and fungicides and pesticides and hybrid seed, and we put out our test plot to prove that religion has nothing to do with agriculture—it belongs to the realm of science.

What we should have said is: This is a God-created and God-sustained world. If we do things God's way, He is responsible for the results. If we do not do things His way, we become responsible for the results. God has enabled us to learn how to put the right things together in accordance with the way He has created the world; and when we do this, God gives us good crops. Science is simply our correct observation of the way God has made the world. There is, indeed, a scientific orderliness about the world, but it had its origin in God's act of creation, and it is maintained by His sustaining power. The results we get from practicing "scientific" agriculture, then, are God's work, not the work of an impersonal force called science.

How does this relate to angels? I have come to the conclusion that, among other functions, angels are God's staff to run the world. We see angels doing such things as giving guidance to people (Genesis 22:11, 15; 31:11, 12), protecting them from danger (Genesis 32:1; 2 Kings 6:17), delivering them (Daniel 3:28; Acts 5:19; 12:7), destroying enemies (Genesis 19:13; 2 Chronicles 32:21; Acts 12:23), providing food for a weary prophet (1 Kings 19:5, 7), and other acts of ministry to "those who will inherit salvation" (Hebrews 1:14). But we also see them controlling what we call the forces of nature in things such as inflicting a plague on the people of Israel (2 Samuel 24:15, 16), perhaps being involved with the plagues visited on the Egyptians and at the least being involved in the pillar of cloud and the pillar of fire which led Israel out of Egypt (Exodus 14:19; Numbers 20:16), killing 185,000 of the enemy (Isaiah 37:36), apparently creating an earthquake to roll the stone from the tomb of Christ (Matthew 28:2), holding back the four winds of the earth (Revelation 7:1), "harm[ing] the land and the sea" (Revelation 7:2), and all the other things angels do in the Book of Revelation.

We are not given a full-blown theology of angels in the Scriptures, but we are told enough to assume that God uses angels to carry out His purposes in the world He created. Far from being an impersonal, material world operating by "natural" law, the world is functionally upheld by the power of God exercised by His authority through angels. Because unbelievers pour scorn on such an idea does not thereby make it untrue. The existence of angels and demons is a fact whether these beings are recognized by science or not. Because one's worldview does not include angels does not prove they aren't there.

The bad-news side of this is that when Lucifer fell and apparently took a third of the angels with him (Revelation 12:4), they became like disgruntled employees who throw sand into the gears of the machines they operate in order to sabotage operations and to "get" the boss. The fallen angels now use their delegated power in the material realm to create alienation and to pervert God's good creation. Human suffering and the destruc-

tive forces in nature were not part of what God pronounced "very good." This is the work of an enemy.

All the angels did not defect, however, and God was
not dethroned. Therefore, pending the time of God's
final execution of judgment on Satan and his angels,
God has set limits on what they can do. They obviously
cannot do whatever they want, or they would long since
have reduced the world to chaos. They operate, as it
were, on a leash. Outside the area covered by the leash
God retains His absolute sovereignty, and our enemy
must secure God's permission to do anything in that
realm. This is illustrated by Satan's bargaining with God
about Job (Job 1:9-12; 2:1-6) and his request to have Peter
to "sift" as wheat (Luke 22:31). Within the leash area,
however, God has chosen to limit the expression of His
sovereignty to the obedience and faith of people. In the
leash area, God's power is still absolute in the sense that
the conditions for the encounter are all set by God, and
someday God will demonstrate His rule by banishing
Satan and his angels to their final judgment (Matthew
25:41; Revelation 20:10).

In the meantime, Satan's attacks on God's children
continue, but faith forms a shield to repulse their attacks
(Ephesians 6:16). It is always God's power which ultimately overcomes these enemies, just as it was always
God who gave victory in the battles between Israel and
pagan nations in the Old Testament. But that power is
released only in response to the obedience and faith of
His people. As Israel always had to engage the enemy in
obedience to God's instructions before God moved in to
defeat their enemy, so we release God's power against our
spiritual enemies through our obedience and faith.
When Israel did not obey and did not exercise faith, the
enemy was allowed to prevail over God's people (see, for
example, Judges 3:7, 8, 12). The same principles operate

today in our spiritual warfare as with Israel in their warfare.

The Realm of People and Things

The issue in this battle is always the glory of God, and the primary battlefield is the third of the realms of being— namely, that of human beings and, closely associated with the human population, the rest of the created world. The creation was designed to declare the glory of God (Psalm 19), and people were created and re-created in order that they might be to the praise of His glory (Ephesians 1:6, 12). Satan and his forces have tried, whenever possible, to mar the reflection of God's glory in nature by introducing enmity, perversion, and even catastrophe into this realm (cf. Romans 8:19-21). They seek every way possible to keep God's people from doing whatever they do to the glory of God (1 Corinthians 10:31). Their primary tactic is the lies they tell about the character of God and about our relationship to Him.

We need to see the secularization of our society as an attack on the very character of God; and we need to see that when we as Christians operate within a secularized worldview, we contribute to that process.

CHAPTER THREE

THE POWER AND THE GLORY

The Old Testament Model

The scene on Mount Carmel was dramatic, to say the least. Elijah had challenged the prophets of Baal to an open contest—a power encounter—to determine who was the true God. For hours the prophets of Baal had been going through their ceremonial antics, with no sign of an answer from Baal. Elijah chided them and urged them to "Shout louder!" When it seemed clear that Baal would not answer, Elijah prepared his sacrifice, had it drenched with water, and then prayed:

> "O LORD, God of Abraham, Isaac and Israel, let it be known today that you are God in Israel and that I am your servant and have done all these things at your command. Answer me, O LORD, answer me, so these people will know that you, O LORD, are God, and that you are turning their hearts back again." (1 Kings 18:36, 37)

The Lord answered Elijah with fire from Heaven to consume the sacrifice and, for good measure, "the wood, the stones and the soil, and also licked up the water in the trench" (v. 38). When the people witnessed this demonstration of God's power, "they fell prostrate and cried, 'The LORD—he is God! The LORD—he is God!'" (v. 39).

God has chosen to reveal His glory through acts of power—some of them of the dramatic type on Mount Carmel, and some of them in the routines of daily life in the form of power to live above one's circumstances. The glory of God is the fundamental issue in any situation, however, and power is only a means to that end.

A primary focus of this book, as should be true for all of the Church, is the Great Commission—the responsibility laid on the Church by our Lord to make disciples in every tribe and nation under Heaven. The salvation of the lost and the bringing of believers to freedom and fullness in Christ are primary objectives for God's people. As important as they are, however, they are not the basic issue. The basic issue is the glory of God. Believers who do all that they do to the glory of God are the kind of witnesses who bring others to faith. So Jesus, in His High Priestly prayer in John 17, prayed, "I have brought you glory on earth by completing the work you gave me to do" (John 17:4). We must therefore begin with the conviction that if God is glorified before the world, He will draw people to Himself.

The Old Testament is most helpful in understanding this. God organized the camp of the nation of Israel with the Tabernacle in the center. In the center of the Tabernacle was the Most Holy Place, with the Ark of the Covenant and the mercy seat. Standing over the Most Holy Place was always the pillar of cloud or the pillar of fire—the *shekinah* glory. Thus the glory of God was always the focus of the camp of Israel. It was God's purpose to demonstrate and declare His glory to the nations through His own nation Israel. So He placed a visible reminder of His glory at the center of Israel as a nation, and He placed Israel in the center of the other nations as as means of revealing His glory to them. When Israel kept this perspective on its identity and mission, God did indeed demonstrate His glory in them, primarily through displays of power. He was, as Wright puts it, a "God who acts."[1] The experience of the spies sent into Jericho is a case in point. Rahab told them:

> "We have heard how the LORD dried up the water of the Red Sea for you when you came out of Egypt, and what you did to Sihon and Og, the two kings of the Amorites east of the Jordan, whom you completely destroyed. When we heard of it, our hearts sank and everyone's courage failed because of you, for the LORD your God is God in heaven above and on the earth below." (Joshua 2:10, 11)

God's mighty acts of power on behalf of His people spoke very loudly to their enemies. We frequently read that God did what He did so that the world would know that Yahweh is God (1 Samuel 17:46; 1 Kings 18:36, 37; 20:13).

This principle is involved in the account of Ben-Hadad's attack on Samaria in the days of Elisha. After an initial defeat at the hands of Israel, Ben-Hadad was advised concerning Israel, "Their gods are gods of the hills. That is why they were too strong for us. But if we fight them on the plains, surely we will be stronger than they." To this Yahweh replied, "Because the Arameans think the LORD is a god of the hills and not a god of the valleys, I will deliver this vast army into your hands, and *you will know that I am the Lord*" (1 Kings 20:23, 28, italics added).

Not only was God's glory demonstrated in His mighty acts, but Israel also sang of God's glory in their

Psalms, and their prophets declared His glory as well. The writings of David and Isaiah are prime examples of this. David had a unique relationship with God, and he reflects his understanding of God when he says, "Declare his glory among the nations, his marvelous deeds among all peoples" (Psalm 96:3). Proclamation ("Declare his glory") and demonstration ("his marvelous deeds") go hand in hand—a principle we also see clearly demonstrated in the ministry of Jesus. James Kallas has an especially helpful discussion of this in his book *The Significance of the Synoptic Miracles*.[2] He argues convincingly that the demonstration of Jesus' power over demons and His ability to do miracles were not just to validate His identity and message; they were actually part of His message. Victory over the demons was evidence of the presence of the Kingdom of God (Matthew 12:28); and the work He began in relation to this Kingdom, we are to continue.

Isaiah had a clear view of the universality and sovereignty of God, reflected especially in passages like chapters 40 and 45. Isaiah was the prophet on duty when Sennacherib laid siege to Jerusalem in the days of King Hezekiah, and it was Isaiah who sent God's graphic word to Sennacherib:

> Because you rage against me
>   and because your insolence has reached my ears,
> I will put my hook in your nose
>   and my bit in your mouth,
> and I will make you return
>   by the way you came.
> (Isaiah 37:29)

The conflict between Israel and the nations is one of the main themes of the Old Testament. From the perspective of the casual observer, it appears to be the usual armed conflict between enemies over a variety of issues. Closer attention to the Scriptural record indicates, however, that victory or defeat was always a matter of God's intervention based on the faith and obedience of Israel. They could go against the enemy with the military odds stacked against them and win decisively (e.g., Judges 6, 7; 2 Chronicles 20), or they could have what appeared to be convincing military superiority and lose (e.g., Joshua 7; Isaiah 30:1-5). The issue was always the faith and obedience of Israel. When they acted on the basis of the true character of God and the reliability of His promises and of their true identity as the people of God, God gave the victory. So God says through the psalmist:

> If my people would but listen to me,
>   if Israel would but follow my ways,
> how quickly would I subdue their enemies
>   and turn my hand against their foes!
> (Psalm 81:13, 14)

And what does this have to do with the subject of spiritual warfare defined as conflict with demonic powers? Precisely this: the gods of the nations were in reality fallen angels masquerading as gods, bringing people into bondage to them by keeping them ignorant of the truth about Yahweh. The real issue was between God and the gods, not just between the people in the nation of Israel and the people in the other nations. This is why the battles were always won or lost on the basis of spiritual power, not military power.

Glory, Worship, and Service

An implication of this is the principle that acceptable service is always based on acceptable worship; true worship will always lead to true service. There may be activities on the part of God's people which are called worship, but which are totally unacceptable to God because they are not a response to the true character of God; thus they do not result in the worshipers carrying out the purposes of God. Isaiah 1:10-20 is dramatic testimony to this. It is correct to say that worship is the reasonable and proper response to God by man and that one of the tests of true worship is whether it leads to service.

If we have really been in God's presence, as David obviously had been before writing Psalm 138, worship will be the natural response to that encounter. Listen to David:

> I will praise you, O LORD, with all my heart;
>   before the "gods" I will sing your praise.
> I will bow down toward your holy temple
>   and will praise your name
> for your love and your faithfulness,
>   for you have exalted above all things
> your name
>   and your word.
> (vv. 1, 2)

Note that David seems to see his worship, in this instance at least, in the context of spiritual warfare when he talks about praising Yahweh "before the 'gods.'" Paul tells us that their gods were really demons (1 Corinthians 10:19, 20), and that seems to be implied in Psalm 106:36, 37 as well:

> They worshiped their idols,
>   which became a snare to them.
> They sacrificed their sons
>   and their daughters to demons.

But worship is not an end in itself as long as we are still on earth. God is certainly worthy to be worshiped apart from any other consideration; there is no motive for worship needed on our part other than a realization of the greatness and glory of God. But being with God at this level of intimacy brings us into touch with God's perspective on the world and with His real concerns. Further, if we don't respond with a commitment to doing all that we do to the glory of God, we have left the act of worship incomplete. Unless we reflect the sovereignty of God in all that we do, we in life deny what we affirm in the so-called time of worship.

In the second stanza of Psalm 138, David immediately reflects the great universal concern of God when he prays:

> May all the kings of the earth
> praise you, O LORD,
> when they hear the words of your mouth.
> May they sing of the ways of the LORD,
> for the glory of the LORD is great.
> (vv. 4, 5)

Notice that the reason for this prayer is that "the glory of the LORD is great." So worship, a response to the glory of God, is a natural and necessary foundation for and motivation to world evangelization. That which is called worship but which does not eventuate in prayer for and involvement in giving expression to God's great love for the world and His desire to see people from all nations come to repentance (John 3:16; 2 Peter 3:9) is probably a man-made substitute for worship rather than a genuine encounter with Yahweh. And service, even missionary service, which is not rooted in worship is likely to fare poorly when tested with fire (1 Corinthians 3:12-15; Matthew 7:22, 23). Our tendency to focus on methods, media, strategies, techniques, formulas, and the like betrays our failure to root our ministries in a reliance upon and demonstration of the power of God. Not that the other things are wrong. I just think Jesus would say what He did about the relation between showing mercy and tithing: "You should have practiced the latter, without neglecting the former" (Matthew 23:23).

Power or Glory

If glory is the issue at stake, why don't we talk about glory encounter rather than power encounter? There is a very good reason for this. Satan cannot compete at the level of glory. Any aspects about him which are or were glorious came from a reflected glory and not from any quality of his own. The glory of God, however, derives from qualities in His very nature and thus depends on no source higher or other than Himself. His creative and sustaining power evidenced in our universe and taken as a whole only begins to define God's glory. At best Satan's acts are deceptive shows of power or counterfeits of God's mighty acts in order to impress and lead astray a people whose perceptions have been badly distorted by sin.

Without the ability to create, Satan cannot begin to compete with God on the level of glory. But he does have power to manipulate that which God has created, and gullible human beings who have lost touch with the real power of God are rather easily impressed by any show of power that is supra-natural. In animistic societies the shows of power may be negative as often as positive; but that there is power involved is not a debatable point with the animists. A missionary who does not have a gospel that involves a demonstrable power greater than the power those with animistic belief systems already know will either get a cool reception or will produce a syncretistic Christianity in which converts continue to go to their traditional sources of power while maintaining a façade of Christianity.

In reality it is our own syncretism which has produced the syncretism on the mission fields. We are shocked when we hear that a candidate for bishop of an evangelical church mothered by American missionaries went to the local magician to secure a charm to enhance his chances of winning the election for bishop. And I am assured by those on the scene researching this phenomenon that such practices are very common.

But why does this happen? I suggest that it is because we Western missionaries do not take a functional belief in spiritual power and in spirit beings with us when we go to the field. We were socialized into a secular approach to the world more deeply than any of us want to admit, and we are therefore as syncretistic from the secular end of the spectrum as animists are from the end where people see spirits and spiritual power behind everything that happens.

So, in the absence of a functional Christian approach to spiritual power, demonic forces can engage in a power encounter with reasonably good results. Christians too often respond to power-encounter situations with fear rather than with confidence in the power of God and the power of the Cross.

True or Counterfeit Power

The problem is, then, that not only do we not provide the contextualized theology and functional faith to deal with the animistic end of the spectrum, we may become rather easy prey for Satan's demonstrations of power in our own cultural setting. We are like those spoken of in Hebrews 5 who ought to be teachers but rather need to go back to the basics. The context there is the essentials of salvation and the Christian life, and there is little that is more fundamental than worldview when it comes to putting Christian truth into practice in the world. We, however, are often not among those "who by constant use have trained themselves to distinguish good from evil" (Hebrews 5:14) in this area.

For some, the question is whether any of what appear to be supra-natural shows of power by demons are actually real, or whether they are simply trickery by persons who know how to create illusions. Given our propensity for easy answers and for polar positions, we tend to solve this problem by relegating all apparently supernatural shows of power by demons to the realm of magic or illusion and to assume anything supernatural which seems to produce something good is from God. It is probably obvious by this time that I am not among those who say that Satan and demons are incapable of manipulating the physical world (at least within what we earlier referred to as the "leash area"), nor that the apparently supra-natural results are produced by human trickery.

There can, for example, be little doubt that there is sometimes a connection between demonic activity and disease. For example, Neil Anderson tells about a young lady who came to him with symptoms which medical authorities diagnosed as multiple sclerosis. In talking with her he discovered that in a time of discouragement and self-pity she had asked God for a "thorn in the flesh," thinking that this would make her more spiritual. It is not the function of a thorn in the flesh to make one spiritual, so God could not answer that prayer. She unwittingly had asked for a "messenger of Satan," and Satan answered her request. When she renounced this prayer and prayed for the removal of any influence by Satan, the symptoms of multiple sclerosis disappeared.[3]

I am aware that many would propose very different explanations for this "spontaneous remission of symptoms." The point is, the remission was not spontaneous; it was in direct response to renouncing a previous invitation to Satan to place a "thorn" in the person. The interworking of the emotional, spiritual, and physical aspects of human life are admittedly intricate, and it is difficult to identify which one may be predominant in any given situation. The problem in many cases is that our spiritual nature is ignored in dealing with human suffering. Since, however, the real person is essentially a spiritual being in the image of God, there is no part of life which can be rightly treated as not related to the spiritual nature or to the spirit world. Our secularized worldview, which at best treats the spiritual realm as "other-worldly" and not necessarily related to the physical body, has often eliminated an essential element in the healing process. It has also allowed Satan to use his limited power to achieve results out of proportion to the power he has.

At this point I simply want to establish my position that nothing has changed since the days of Jesus when it comes to demonic activity affecting the human body and human life in general. I assume the New Testament is accurate when it states that one-third of the healings by Jesus recorded in the Gospels involved the casting out of demons.

Demons are fallen angels, and it is consistent with the nature of angels for demons to function in the way they do. When they fell, God could have withdrawn their power or consigned them immediately to the Abyss. Instead, He chose to show His power over them by taking the evil they would do in the lives of people and using it to build strength into their lives. In similar fashion, He did not withdraw His image from His human children when they sinned. He, rather, demonstrated His grace by providing redemption for us and fitting us for glory in spite of the worst the enemy can do to us.

Power to Live to the Glory of God

As we said earlier, spiritual warfare does not begin with overt demonic activity. It begins the minute we set our wills to move from the power of Satan to God and walk in His truth. The bolder our steps of faith and obedience, the more the enemy is motivated to try to get us off-track. His aim is to neutralize us in terms of effective witness—to keep us from living lives that bring glory to God.

Our position in the battle will need to be defensive as well as offensive. We must be prepared to defend ourselves against demonic attack, and we must be equipped to press the battle against the enemy by invading his territory through various forms of Christian ministry. But our supreme concern must be that "whether [we] eat or drink or whatever [we] do, [we] do it all for the glory of God" (1 Corinthians 10:31). If Satan can cause God's servants to live essentially powerless lives which are not to the glory of God, he wins another battle in this warfare. On the other hand, when we demonstrate the power to live in significant victory over the circumstances of life and over the attacks of the enemy, then we live to the glory of God, and the unsaved and hurting people around us will seek us out to find the source of our power.

It was not only in Old Testament times that the glory of God drew the nations to Him. This still works today, and the demonstration of His glory through power to meet every circumstance of life is basic to our witness to the world.

CHAPTER FOUR

SPIRITUAL POWER GOOD AND BAD

AN OLD AND FAMILIAR saying contends that "power corrupts, and absolute power corrupts absolutely." This fear of power doesn't help us when it comes to talking about power in the spiritual realm. As with most generalizations, however, this one needs a good bit of qualification. To begin with, only God has absolute power, and it does not corrupt Him. In the second place, power is an essential part of life; properly used, it does not corrupt. It is true, of course, that almost any kind of power can be misused, but it is not the power itself which corrupts. It is a fascination with, an inordinate desire for, or a misuse of power which corrupts.

The Problem of Balance

Since power is essential to life, as we tried to show in Chapter One, we can be sure Satan will attempt to pervert the use of power in some way. This leads to what has become a virtual philosophy of life for me—one I developed a good many years ago and have sought to follow since. Its relevance to the subject at hand is fairly obvious. It may be stated as follows: The Christian life is the exciting process of trying to keep your balance.

Behind this philosophy is the premise that evil is always the perversion of a good. When God finished creating the world He pronounced it "very good" (Genesis 1:31). There was no evil in the world as it came from the hand of God. Satan came on the scene later with his jealousy of God and began to scheme as to how he could pervert what God had made good. He is not a creator, so he could not produce a competing world. He could only try to undo what God had done.

Whittaker Chambers, in an article entitled "The Devil," gives the account of an imaginary conversation with Satan in which Satan is boasting of the way he has led people to use their abilities to bring the world to the point of self-destruction. Chambers then asks him, "Just what do you get out of it?," to which Satan replies:

> My friend, you do not understand the devil's secret. But since shamelessness is part of my pathos, there is no reason why I should not tell you. The devil is sterile. I possess the will to create (hence my pride), but I am incapable of creating (hence my envy). And with an envy raised to such power as mortal minds can feel, I hate the Creator and His creation. My greatest masterpiece is never more than a perversion—an ingenious disordering of another's grand design, a perversion of order into chaos, of life into death. Why? . . . Perhaps it is simply, as every craftsman knows, that nothing enduring, great or small, can ever be created without love. But I am as incapable of love as I am of goodness.[1]

Chambers makes the point well. Perversion is the essence of Satan's work. He has the power of an angel, but only the power of an angel—not the power of God.

In the final analysis, whatever power Satan has is God's power which was delegated to him as an angel. Just as God has not withdrawn from us the ability to misuse our power to subdue the earth, so He has not withdrawn from the fallen angels their angelic power. They simply use that power now to frustrate God's good purposes for creation rather than to further those purposes.

One of Satan's perversions relates to the concept of power. He will deceive some people into seeking power from wrong motivations and into using it for wrong purposes. This is what leads to the idea that power corrupts. This seems to be especially true in relation to spiritual power. Satan has been unusually successful in getting some people to define the Christian life, and especially church services, as a constant diet of spectacular demonstrations of spiritual power. The problem is, the question is not often asked as to where the power is coming from or whether the results are in harmony with the teachings of Scripture. On the other hand, the devil will get other people to overreact to the misuse of power and to accept a relatively powerless life as normal.

Revival movements have often been accompanied by genuine demonstrations of power such as trembling under conviction of sin. It is also true, however, that Satan has almost always tried to subvert revival movements by imitating such physical manifestations and diverting attention to those manifestations and away from the true spiritual work being done.

The easy way to avoid that extreme is simply to withdraw from a concern with the demonstration of spiritual power. But that also is a part of Satan's plan. A powerless Church serves his purposes very well. Few arguments carry more weight with unbelievers than the one based on the impotence of the Church in the realm of spiritual power. Satan doesn't worry much about religious activity as such. Activity which is not bringing people from his kingdom into God's and which is not freeing people from the bondages into which he brings some of God's children poses no threat to Satan at all. Such powerless activity may, in fact, serve his cause well.

Related to this is the whole subject of demons. On the one hand there are those who want to see demons as the cause behind every human problem and who propose simplistic answers to complex human situations. The animists, for example, ascribe a maximum of causation to the spirit world, seeing spirits where there are none. In our own society there are those who want to solve every human problem by casting out demons. Anger, for example, is always thought to be a demon—if the demon of anger is cast out, the anger will go away. The more basic issue of forgiveness is unfortunately bypassed. More frequently, however, the tendency has been to ascribe no causation to the spirit world. Demonic involvement is not even a consideration in analyzing human problems. It is as C. S. Lewis put it so well:

> There are two equal and opposite extremes into which our race can fall about the devils [demons]. One is to disbelieve in their existence. The other is to believe, and to feel an excessive and unhealthy interest in them. They themselves are equally pleased by both errors and hail a materialist or a magician with the same delight.[2]

From the point of view of either extreme, the Biblical balance-point will seem pretty far away, perhaps even "out in left field." This is why I say the Christian life is the exciting process of trying to keep your balance. Sometimes I say it is the exciting "struggle" for balance, because I believe this is very much a part of the spiritual warfare in which we are engaged. Someone has put it this way:

The devil . . . always sends errors into the world in pairs—pairs of opposites. And he always encourages us to spend a lot of time thinking which is the worse. You see why, of course. He relies on our extra dislike of the one error to draw us gradually into the opposite one. . . . We have to keep our eyes on the goal and go straight through between both errors. We have no other concern than that with either of them.[3]

To add to the confusion, everyone likes to think that his or her view is the balanced one. The problem often comes from a wrong definition of the extremes. To those at one extreme, the center seems like the other extreme, and the apparent balance is still pretty far in one direction.

By this I do not mean to imply that we should always be in the middle of the road on any issue because, as I have just said, the ends of the spectrum may not have been correctly defined. Nor do I mean that everyone will be at precisely the same place on every issue, or that balance is a mold into which everyone must fit. I do believe, however, that large segments of the Church have become so accustomed to operating with no demonstration of spiritual power that they are bothered by any demonstration. Thus a balanced view would be labeled extreme.

With this rather lengthy introduction to give perspective to our discussion of the topic at hand, let us move on to look at the basis of the Christian confidence for victory in spiritual warfare.

God's Role versus Satan's Role

We have defined the primary combatants in this conflict as God, the holy angels, and believers on one side, and Satan, the fallen angels, and unbelievers on the other. The question may then be asked, "On what basis do

Christians presume to enter into combat with Satan and his forces? Is this not a conflict between God and Satan which God will fight on the basis of His sovereignty without the involvement of Christians on earth?"

There is certainly a sense in which God and Satan are the primary combatants, and it is indeed true that God does exercise control from His position of sovereignty. But in Old Testament times God normally did not give victory to Israel with the army sitting in camp, even though He was the one who always provided the margin of triumph in any battle with the enemies of Israel (see Psalm 44:3). Likewise, today He is the one who provides the power needed in our spiritual warfare. But God did not provide the power for Israel apart from their faith and obedience, and He does not provide the power today apart from our steps of faith and obedience.

Israel always had to encounter the enemy in some fashion. In the same way, it is God's power today which provides the margin of victory in our encounters with the spiritual enemy, but He almost always gives us, His children, something to do in the battle. We cannot take for granted our protection from the enemy without active faith and courageous obedience on our part.

God's Missionary Strategy

God's strategy in the Old Testament was to place His one special nation, Israel, in the midst of the other nations, and through Israel to demonstrate His glory to the peoples around them. In this manner He would reveal Himself to those nations. In the New Testament the strategy changes. God now has ordained that the Church be planted in every nation and that His truth be proclaimed and His glory be demonstrated by the Church within each nation as the means of drawing people to Him. But the Church is not only to be His witness to the nation in which it is located; it is to have a missionary focus from its very inception and to participate in the work of planting the Church in nations and among peoples where no church exists, both through prayer and through the active sending of missionaries.

The heart of the commission to do this is, "make disciples of all nations" (Matthew 28:19). That is like a commanding officer ordering his troops to liberate prisoners of war from the enemy. In order to do that, it is necessary to overcome the power by which the enemy holds those prisoners. The unit with which I served in the Second World War had the experience of liberating many prisoners and slave laborers. In order to do so, we had to overpower the troops that held them. It would have been folly to suppose that the enemy was going to allow us to invade his territory and free the captives without resistance.

Engaging our spiritual enemy in an offensive manner is as much a part of carrying out the commission given to the Church as engaging the human enemy was a part of the commission of Israel to liberate the Promised Land and as our commission as the Allied Forces in World War II was to liberate enemy-held territory. I used to think it was only missionaries overseas who encountered the enemy directly. We will see later how every obedient believer is involved in this offensive warfare.

The Spiritual Authority Behind the Commission

Such an invasion of enemy territory is not undertaken on a person-by-person initiative. It is done under the command of the One who has ultimate authority in the Kingdom of God. This is why Jesus began His Great Commission to the Church with the words, "All author-

ity in heaven and on earth has been given to me"
(Matthew 28:18). It is because He has such authority that
He can commission us to go into this battle. And Paul
makes it clear that the primary battle is against spiritual,
not human, forces (Ephesians 6:12). The human dimensions are always involved, but it is our encounter with
spiritual forces which determines who wins in any given
spiritual skirmish. The reason so many churches are seeing so few prisoners liberated is that they are fighting the
wrong enemy, or they are fighting with the wrong
weapons.

This is one of the fallacies of some who espouse
Liberation Theology. They say that the social and political structures are demonic, but then they propose that
the way to bring them down is with social, political, and
even military action. If these structures are really
demonic, they will be brought down by spiritual
weapons, not by the weapons of the world. Some structures do in fact need changing, but good structures do
not make bad people good, though good people can
redeem even bad structures. The most basic consideration, then, is not in changing the structures, but in bringing people into touch with the power which enables
them to rise above any set of circumstances. The Church
in Communist China is a prime example of this. Without
overthrowing an oppressive political system, one of the
greatest revival movements in history has taken place; a
powerful Church exists in spite of the system.

This is not to say that we shouldn't work for the
establishment of justice. It is to say that demonic forces,
whether those in a system (and the people who operate
the system) like the government of Communist China or
those that attack us personally, must be overcome with
the power that comes from God, not the weapons of the
flesh or of the world.

God's power, then, is an essential for victory in this

warfare. There really is no other source of power for the believer. There is none which we have in and of ourselves. When God is alive in us and working through us, we have the power to overcome all the attacks of the enemy. His power is good and not something to be feared or shunned.

C H A P T E R   F I V E

THE POWER OF THE CROSS

THE UNIT IN WHICH I served in the Second World War was given the assignment to "mop up" in the Ruhr pocket. The main lines of battle had moved well to the east, and the outcome of the war was not seriously in doubt. There was no doubt at all about our ability to overcome the resistance we faced in our assignment. It was still war, however. Real guns and real ammunition were being used. People were still being hurt and even killed. We had no fear, however, that the enemy was going to launch any major offensive against us that would threaten our position of military superiority.

This illustrates a very unique fact about the spiritual war in which we are engaged—namely, the outcome is never in doubt. The decisive battle has already been fought and won. That battle was fought and won at the Cross. The Resurrection followed immediately as a demonstration of the power to be made available to the Church for its battle with Satan and his forces (Ephesians 1:19, 20). I believe that this victory is at least part of what Jesus had in mind when He called out from the Cross, "It is finished" (John 19:30). The truth of victory is also stated clearly by Paul in Colossians 2:15, "And having disarmed the powers and authorities, he made a public spectacle of them, triumphing over them by the cross."

In the economy of God, Jesus was, of course, "the Lamb that was slain from the creation of the world" (Revelation 13:8). In the eternity of God there has never been a time when Satan was not under the control of God. But from the perspective of time, as viewed by people on the earth, something significant happened at the Cross. Prior to the Cross we operated on the basis of types and "shadows" (Colossians 2:16, 17; Hebrews 8:5; 10:1). But since the Incarnation and death of Christ, we operate on the basis of historic fact. If there was any basis for question before Calvary, there is certainly none now. At the Cross God allowed Christ to become sin for us (2 Corinthians 5:21) so Satan could exact the death penalty on Christ (though it is also true that Jesus chose this role; it was not forced on Him—see John 10:17, 18). But God used that event to demonstrate that He is able to take the worst Satan can do and turn it into victory. The Cross was supposed to be a victory for Satan and a defeat for God. Instead, the Cross now has become the Christian symbol of victory. It is displayed proudly because there the enemy was defeated once and for all.

The sentence of death on Satan has been pronounced. It simply has not been finally executed. Jesus tells us clearly that "eternal fire" has been "prepared for the devil and his angels" (Matthew 25:41). In Revelation we are told that at some point in the future the devil will be "thrown into the lake of burning sulfur" (Revelation 20:10).

The writer to the Hebrews speaks of what happened at the Cross this way:

Since the children have flesh and blood, he [Jesus] too shared in their humanity so that by his death he might destroy him who holds the power of death—

that is, the devil—and free those who all their lives were held in slavery by their fear of death. (2:14, 15)

In Revelation 12 we read about the war in Heaven. Wherever you place this in your eschatological chronology of events, the fact of victory is again recorded, and the message to the inhabitants of the earth (v. 12) is:

But woe to the earth and the sea,
    because the devil has gone down to you!
He is filled with fury,
    because he knows that his time is short.

Satan knows he is defeated. He knows his time is limited. Earlier we are told that the people on earth "overcame him by the blood of the Lamb and by the word of their testimony" (v. 11). The enemy uses two bases for attacking us. One is sin on our part, but Christ, through the Cross, has provided forgiveness and cleansing for all our sin. If we agree with God about our sin and His remedy for it, Satan can no longer hold us in bondage through guilt.

The other principal basis of attack is self. His aim is always to get us to be self-centered instead of God-centered. But self also goes to the Cross with Christ, and God's children do not "love their lives so much as to shrink from death" (Revelation 12:11). So if I have been crucified with Christ (Galatians 2:20), if my self has gone to the Cross and I daily reckon my self dead to the demands of that old nature, the Cross is the basis of my victory. It remains only for me to appropriate that victory by faith. That is why Paul says, "May I never boast except in the cross of our Lord Jesus Christ, through which the world has been crucified to me, and I to the world" (Galatians 6:14).

Donald Jacobs, the Mennonite anthropologist/missiologist, says that great harm has been done to the cause of Christ because demonology and the victory view of the atonement have not been considered respectable during the modern missions era.[1] John Newport, in a paper given at the Christian Medical Society symposium on the demonic, held at Notre Dame University in 1975, said of this:

> Fortunately . . . the victory, or triumphant view of the atonement is coming back into its own. The sacrificial, substitutionary, propitiatory and redemptive views of the atonement all have validity. However, the triumphant view must take its proper place. Much of the New Testament . . . has to do with the power of Satan and demons, and this victory view should be seen as quite important.[2]

Newport cites George Ladd's interpretation of Colossians 2:15, saying that Ladd

> understands the verse to mean that Christ has disarmed the spiritual powers, stripping them of their insignia of rank or of their arms. Thus the verse states that by His death Christ triumphed over His spiritual enemies, winning a divine triumph over the cosmic powers.[3]

This view of the Cross forms the primary basis for the exercise of power over the forces of the enemy. The Christ who achieved this victory and confirmed it by His resurrection is the one who said, "All authority in heaven and on earth has been given to me. Therefore go and make disciples of all nations" (Matthew 28:18, 19). We are delegated by this commission to enforce the victory won at the Cross in our ministry of planting the Church around the world and in our daily lives. Our failure to claim that victory when confronted by entrenched forces of evil has contributed significantly to the great problems of syncretism now plaguing the Church almost everywhere in the world.

Today, however, large segments of the Church seem to have lost sight of this critical truth about the Cross and the clear basis for victory which it provides. With the secularization of our worldview, the reality of spiritual warfare has almost disappeared from our thinking; and rather than risk the scorn of our peers, we seek to have as little to do with the world of demons as possible, being content to leave them in the realm of theory or theology. To bring them into everyday life would be to risk ridicule; and that is something none of us likes and very few of us handle well.

The World, the Flesh, and the Devil

Some will want to point out that some of the passages cited do not say anything about demons. They speak of the world or of the flesh. How can we use those verses to talk about spiritual warfare?

Our Western worldview gets involved here once again. We have a strong tendency to want to analyze everything and place the parts in neat, mutually exclusive categories. So we ask questions like, How do you know whether it is the world, the flesh, or the devil? My response is that most situations will involve some of each element to some extent. Notice how Paul treats these three aspects of evil in Ephesians 2:

> As for you, you were dead in your transgressions and sins, in which you used to live when you followed the ways of this *world* and of the ruler of the kingdom of the air [the *devil*], the spirit who is now at work in those who are disobedient. All of us also lived among

them at one time, gratifying the cravings of our sinful nature [the *flesh*, Greek *sarx*], and following its desires and thoughts. (vv. 1-3)

The three elements are treated as working together so closely that you cannot talk about one without talking about the other. The flesh is the earthly qualities about us which enable us to respond to temptation. The world is the milieu in which we live and which is under the control of "the ruler of the kingdom of the air." Satan and his demons know what fleshly parts of us are especially vulnerable, and they use the stimuli of the world around us to arouse sinful thoughts in us. The Devil would be a fool not to try to take advantage of the world and the flesh in his aim to destroy us. One does not have to stretch the Scriptures to see him at work in all of these relationships.

Our Position in Christ

There is another important factor involved in our position of victory, and that is the relationship to God which comes about as a result of our being brought into His family. The beginning of this new relationship is often portrayed through the metaphor of birth. In Galatians (4:4-7) and in Ephesians (1:5) Paul uses the metaphor of adoption to help us understand this new relationship. He says that we were slaves, but God adopted us into His family and gave us "the full rights of sons" (Galatians 4:5). This metaphor is full of meaning. Two of my four children are mine by adoption. I had nothing to do with their conception or birth, and yet their birth certificate today says that I am their father. Frankly, when the new birth certificates came I was surprised. I didn't know that adoption was carried that far.

That is the concept behind Paul's prayer, beginning

in verse 15 of Ephesians 1. One of the petitions in that prayer is that these young Christians may know "the riches of his glorious inheritance in the saints" (v. 18). The fact was, they needed to learn to think like saints rather than sinners and like princes and princesses rather than like commoners. They needed to recognize that the resources of their adoptive Father were available to them. He was no longer a distant monarch with whom they would have to have an appointment to talk. He was their Father, and they were welcome in the throne room any time they needed to talk with Him.

When I adopted our two older children (a girl and a boy), I went before a judge who said to me, "Do you understand that these children must be equally your heirs with any children who may be born to you and your wife?" My ready reply was, "I understand that, sir, and I gladly accept it." So those two children have as much right to my name and to my resources as the two children who were born into our family. Our adoption into the family of God brings us into the same relationship with Him as my adopted children have to me. Paul tells us clearly that because we are God's children we are "heirs of God and co-heirs with Christ" (Romans 8:17).

One of Satan's chief tactics in his attacks on us is to keep us from understanding the implications of this new relationship with our Heavenly Father. Through the Cross, Satan's claim on us is completely canceled. Just as my son and daughter's birth certificates make no mention of their biological father but list me alone as their father, so we are spiritually children of God alone. Our enemy no longer has any claim on us. In fact, with the resources of God at my disposal, I am more than a match for the enemy in his attempts to bring me into bondage to him again.

Being an heir not only means that someday we will receive an inheritance—our family relationship gives us unique privileges right now. We may act in the name of our Father in a way those not in the family may not. The seven sons of Sceva discovered the negative aspect of this truth the hard way. When they tried to use the name of Jesus to cast out demons without first becoming God's children through faith in Christ, the demons overpowered them (Acts 19:13-16).

This concept of our family relationship to God can be seen in the exchange between Jesus and the seventy-two in Luke 10. They had been out on their fieldwork assignment, and things had obviously gone rather well. In fact, on their return they reported excitedly to Jesus that "even the demons submit to *us* in your name" (italics added). Jesus answered,

> "I saw Satan fall like lightning from heaven. I have given you authority to trample on snakes and scorpions, and to overcome all the power of the enemy; nothing will harm you. However, do not rejoice that the spirits submit to you, but rejoice that your names are written in heaven." (Luke 10:17-20)

I believe Jesus was saying to them, "You do indeed have the authority to cast out demons—essentially the same authority I have. But don't get all excited about that, as though that marks you out as some special class of super-spiritual persons. Rather, focus on your family relationship to God, because it is that relationship which gives you this authority." Power to resist the devil is not a gift given to a few special believers. It is the privilege and the responsibility of every child of God. This is why James could say, "Submit yourselves . . . to God. [Then] Resist the devil, and he will flee from you" (James 4:7).

Many people struggle with areas of bondage in their lives because they have never clearly identified who they are "in Christ." They depend on their relationships with other people for their sense of identity rather than on their relationship with the Lord. They are trying to live on the basis of Satan's lies rather than on the basis of God's truth. Satan's lies are so deceptive, however, that there is no recognition of where they come from. The degree to which we try to live our lives on the basis of the lies is the degree to which Satan has us in some measure of bondage to him. The truth about our victory in Christ is an essential starting-point for claiming victory in daily life.

Yes, the outcome of the war has already been decided. God has let us read the end of the book. But there are still battles being fought, and we need to be clear about the basis of our claim to victory. For very practical help with these concepts, see Neil Anderson, *Victory over the Darkness* (Regal) and *The Bondage Breaker* (Harvest House).

The Ministry of the Holy Spirit

The Cross provides all the power we need to be victorious in this warfare, but it is the ministry of the Holy Spirit which makes that power effective in our lives. The Cross defeated the enemy and provided the basis for spiritual life for us who believe. The Spirit is that life. When He dwells in us, we have life; when He does not dwell in us, we remain in spiritual death.

It is my understanding of Scripture that we receive the Holy Spirit when we are converted. He baptizes us into the Body of Christ, the Church (1 Corinthians 12:13). Apart from His presence we do "not belong to Christ" (Romans 8:9). The problem is, we are often reluctant to give over the direction of our lives to someone else, even the Spirit of God. We want the "blessings" He can bring, but the issue of authority may be unresolved. As strange as it seems, we have the ability to restrict the operation of the Holy Spirit in our lives so that He cannot do what He would like to do. This is one of the ways we can "grieve the Holy Spirit of God" (Ephesians 4:30). Our hazy concepts of what spirits are and of how they can be involved in the everyday affairs of life contribute to this problem.

To be Spirit-filled, on the other hand, is not to be filled from head to toe with the Spirit. It is to have all areas of life under His direction. This is not a kind of control where we are passive and the Spirit is doing something. It is an active cooperation between our wills and the will of God. It is our response to God with faith and obedience—faith that actively appropriates the promises of God and obedience that walks "according to the Spirit" (Romans 8:1, 4; Galatians 5:25).

The point is, we do not need some special, new experience of the Holy Spirit in order to participate victoriously in spiritual warfare. We simply need to realize who dwells within us and what He can do if permitted to by our faith and obedience.

Consider as an example what is sometimes called a missionary call. God may speak to a person about serving Him as a cross-cultural missionary, but there is resistance to that leading. The struggle goes on for a time, and then, in an act of surrender, all the emotions are released, and the person calls that emotional experience a "call." The real call came a long time before the surrender, and if the issue of Lordship had been faced honestly at that time, there would never have been a crisis experience. Lordship means saying to God, "I give You the prior consent of my will to do whatever You say. If it is to serve You in a high-risk area of ministry, I believe that You are better able to make that decision than I am and that You are abundantly able to give me the resources to do what You ask me to do." Too often our attitude, if not our words, says, "Show me what You want me to do, and I will decide whether I want to do it or not." That is the attitude which makes for crisis experiences.

Similarly, the Holy Spirit has been there all along, ever since the day He made us new creatures in Christ. He has been ready to carry out His plans for us, but we haven't been ready to let Him. The conflict between our wrong beliefs and our self-centered desires on the one hand and the Holy Spirit on the other finally comes to a point of decision which may involve a great experience of emotional release and possibly a demonstration of the power of the Spirit. But if there had never been the conflict, the emotional experience might never have occurred and the demonstration of power would have come much sooner. If we had been more adequately instructed, and if we had been prepared to make a fuller and more intelligent commitment earlier in the conversion-sanctification process, the experience would not have been of a crisis nature.

A related problem, which Satan will try to take advantage of, may be that some people like emotional experiences and try to re-create them on a regular basis. Emotions are a very real and important part of our lives, and we need to know how to live with them. However, we must never allow them to be the criteria for truth or for spiritual maturity or even for the success of a "worship" service.

This brings us back to the realization that in the final analysis it is God who is the primary actor in all of this. Achieving victory over our enemy is not so much something I do as it is something God does through me as His agent. But just as God did not act to give victory over Israel's enemies until Israel took the steps of obedience required by God, so God does not act in the encounters we face until we move in obedience to what He has revealed to us in His Word and through the guidance of His Spirit.

Acts 1:8 makes it clear that there is a vital relationship between the ministry of the Spirit in our lives and
the working of spiritual power. This verse is sometimes
given as a form of the Great Commission, and there is a
sense in which that is correct. But it is actually a declar-
ative sentence, not a command. It states a fact: when the
Holy Spirit comes upon us, we will indeed receive power
and will be witnesses to the ends of the earth. That is the
Spirit's function—to empower us for witness about
Christ among all nations. We may cooperate with Him
in carrying out that purpose, or we may grieve Him by
resisting Him.

Just as many Christians do not reckon on their new
life in Christ, but rather live far below their privileges as
children of God, so others take their criteria for success
and the "good life" from the world rather than from the
Spirit and end up with self-centered lives instead of lives
of service to others. This will obviously hinder the flow
of His power through them, but it does not mean that He
is not there.

The truth is, if I am "in Christ," *I am in Christ*. I don't
get partway in at first and then gradually get all the way
in. I become a "new creation," period. There is nothing
I can do which will make me more justified before God
than I am. If I don't believe that, I will live out a weak
faith. So if the Holy Spirit lives within me, giving me that
new life, it is only my failure to trust Him and to obey
Him that will keep His power from flowing through me.

Conclusion

One of the great needs of the Church today is to bring
the truth about the victory of Christ and of the power of
the Holy Spirit from the realm of theory or professed
belief into the realm of practical experience. We need to
stop allowing fear to motivate us when demons are men-

tioned and begin treating demons like the defeated enemies they are. Satan has often succeeded in getting us to
think that if we so much as study this subject, something
awful may happen to us. The opposite is true. The more
we know about our victory in Christ, and the more we
know about our defeated enemy, the more confident we
will be in the conflict in which we are engaged and
which we cannot avoid. A man I discipled said to me not
long ago, "I was brought up in a good evangelical church
with the usual idea that the safest thing to do with the
subject of Satan and demons is to leave it alone. Study in
that area only generates problems. I have found it to be
just the other way around. I have never been more
confident in my walk with Christ than I am today."
Amen!

C H A P T E R   S I X

SPIRITUAL AUTHORITY

DICK HILLIS, LONGTIME DIRECTOR of Overseas Crusades, was a relatively new missionary in China when a young Chinese soldier came to his door asking, "Is your Christ all-powerful?"

"Of course He is," responded Hillis with no hesitation.

"Good," replied the soldier. "My wife is in the courtyard, and she is demon-possessed. Twice the demon has ordered her to kill herself, once by hanging and once by jumping into the moat. Both times she obeyed him, but I was able to rescue her. However, I do not know what to do now, as I must go back to my battalion. I had heard that Christ was able to heal those who are demon-possessed, and so I have brought her to you."

Hillis's wife was standing with him and tried to encourage him with the truth that "Jesus Christ is the same yesterday and today and forever" (Hebrews 13:8). Hillis's theological education had not equipped him to deal with demons, but he knew he had to do something. So the Hillises and a "Bible woman" (church worker) took the young wife to the women's compound and began praying for her. Hillis says, "I confess that I prayed in doubt, wondering if I would need some special gift of healing." To make matters worse, Hillis says, "the demon-possessed woman would take words from our prayers and make ridiculous poems out of them. . . . She would scream and yell and make fun of what we were doing."

They struggled in prayer for three days with no results. That day the soldier showed up to get his wife, but the missionary asked for more time. The Lord also led him to ask if they had any idols in their home. When the soldier answered that they did, he was told to go and destroy them. The result was that the next morning the demons were complaining that their home had been destroyed. So Hillis knew that the soldier had indeed gotten rid of the idols, but the demons remained in the woman.

Hillis then reports:

> In our reading of the Scriptures, we were going through Ephesians 1 and 2, and God suddenly revealed that we were not only identified with Christ in death and in His resurrection, but that we were "seated with Christ in heavenly places far above principalities and powers"; that we had ascended with Him. Taking this new position, our Christian postmaster, my wife and I sang in the presence of the woman, "There's power in the blood," and then after singing, we commanded the demon to come out of her in the name of Jesus. *She was instantly delivered!*

The young missionary learned two important lessons. The first was the necessity of clearly understanding the believer's position in Christ—seated with Him in the heavenly realms—and the implications of that for our encounter with the enemy. The second was that "it is not enough to pray or to sing, though I believe that Satan hates both prayer and song. We must resist the devil and command that he depart."[1]

Delegated Authority

The question may now rightly be asked, "But what about the exercise of authority? Does a Christian really have any right to exercise spiritual authority over demons?" That was probably the issue in the minds of the seventy-two when they returned from their period of ministry, and Jesus made it very clear that He was giving them the right to use His authority in dealing with the demons. That is also one of the reasons the Great Commission begins with a statement of Jesus' authority. The clear implication is that those who go out to make disciples operate with delegated authority over Satan and demons.

The Use of Authority

Our culture tends to get in the way on this issue, just as it does in relation to the reality of demons in the first place. The exercise of authority has become increasingly suspect as individual rights have come into ascendancy. When one puts the two problems together, there are very few Christians who are prepared to repel enemy attacks or to invade enemy territory with confidence that they have the authority to overcome our spiritual enemy.

If we do meet the enemy, we are apt to do what Dick Hillis did the first time he came face to face with a demon in China. We run to our Father and say, "Father, take care of this big bully for me." If we were really a child, God might do that. But when we are adults, He is more apt to say, "I have delegated to you the authority you need to resist that enemy. Use that authority."

Most of us seem to prefer a state of spiritual infancy rather than spiritual adulthood when it comes to dealing with the enemy. It is like a child who at age four comes running to the parent saying, "Daddy, he hit me," and Daddy goes and gets things straightened out. That is fine at age four; but if that is still going on at age twenty-four, you have a problem. Successful parenting prepares the child to handle conflict as a responsible adult.

So it is with our growing up in the family of God. There are times when we can legitimately go to God and ask Him to handle things for us. But there comes a time when our Heavenly Father says to us, "I have made you in My image with a mind and a will; I have delegated My authority to you. I expect you to use those gifts responsibly. That takes practice, however—so get on with learning by doing. I will no longer do for you what I have equipped you to do."

This principle is involved in Hebrews 5, where the recipients of the letter seem to have chosen spiritual infancy as a perpetual state. The writer says,

> [T]hough by this time you ought to be teachers, you need someone to teach you the elementary truths of God's word all over again. You need milk, not solid food . . . solid food is for the mature, who by constant use have trained themselves to distinguish good from evil. (vv. 12-14)

One of the marks of spiritual maturity is the confidence to resist the enemy with the authority of Christ—indeed, to be confident that that authority is effective against all the host of hell.

Our first experience of dealing with a demonized person was in the form of a direct challenge to us. The young lady had been referred to us by a counselor because her symptoms were simply not yielding to normal Christian counseling. In this case we began by testing her ability to speak in tongues (a spiritual gift often counterfeited by the enemy); and when we asked the spirit giving her the tongue whether it confessed that Jesus Christ was God's Son come in the flesh, a voice quite different from that of this diminutive young lady said, "I'm strong; you can't get me." My answer was, "That's right, I can't. But Christ can, and in His name I command you to leave her." If I were to repeat that situation today, I would probably help the young woman exercise the authority herself, based on her own relationship to Christ. But whether done by the counselor or the counselee, it is imperative that we be prepared to act with authority when necessary.

I readily confess that as I approached that first encounter there were predictable fears. I thought to myself, "I'll really look foolish if nothing happens." When I said to the counselee, "I am not going to be talking to you; I will be addressing any spirit that may be present," it was a strange feeling to be speaking to something or someone I could not see, even though I do this in prayer all the time. It would have been a lot easier just to say, "Well, we will pray for you and ask God to free you from whatever is bothering you." I frankly think that such a prayer would have done little good. I believe a direct encounter was needed. Incidentally, there were a number of other encounters with demons in this person, going back to occult involvement on the part of her mother and grandmother. The point I am making is simply that an approach involving authority is often required.

Policeman Analogy

But, someone asks, what about the passage in Jude which tells us that even Michael "did not dare to bring a slanderous accusation against him [Satan], but said, 'The Lord rebuke you!'" (v. 9). The context here is the problem of men who "reject authority and slander celestial beings" (v. 8). They have already rejected the idea of living under God's authority and are acting on their own assumed authority. That is indeed folly. There is no basis whatsoever for a human being assuming a position of authority based on his or her own identity.

If, however, I am acting as the agent of one who has the ultimate power and therefore has the right to authorize others to act in His behalf on the basis of that power, we have an entirely different situation. John MacMillan, in his little book entitled *The Authority of the Believer*,[2] uses the figure of a policeman to illustrate this relationship. If a man comes to my door and says he would like to search my house, I will probably respond, "And who are you?" If he identifies himself as a neighbor from down the street, I will feel no obligation even to let him in my house.

But if that same man comes to my door dressed in a police uniform and carrying a badge and a search warrant which I deem to be valid, I will not ask him for personal identification. I will relate to him on the basis of his relationship to the authority of the state. In his own identity he has no authority to demand to search my house. However, as a representative of the government he has every right to do so.

Or, to put it another way, a policeman who is assigned to direct traffic at a busy intersection has no *power* to stop the trucks and other vehicles which approach that crossing. It would take a massive physical object to provide power sufficient to stop the huge semi-trailer rigs approaching his post of duty. His delegated *authority*, however, gives him the right to raise his hand and blow his whistle and control the flow of traffic.

Authority is delegated power. Whenever we assume that the right to exercise authority resides in us personally, we are in trouble. No one is competent to exercise authority until he has first learned to live under author-

LINCOLN CHRISTIAN COLLEGE AND SEMINARY

ity. All authority flows from God. This is why James says, "Submit yourselves, then, to God. . . . [Then] Resist the devil, and he will flee from you" (4:7).

Another factor of significance is that it does not matter whether the policeman is one week out of the police academy or a twenty-year veteran. The badge has exactly the same amount of authority behind it. This is why the seventy-two in Luke 10 could cast out demons even though it was their first ministry experience. The twenty-year veteran may have much more wisdom and skill in the use of his authority, and he is more apt to be assigned to difficult cases, but the authority is the same.

There will always be dangers with the possible misuse of the concept of authority. As we have noted, a person may come to believe that the authority actually resides in himself or herself. Thus, in dealing with demons it is important that we understand clearly that we operate on delegated authority.

Another problem with the use of authority is that it easily degenerates into using a formula. Some people seem to think that if they just say the right words using the name of Jesus, they are guaranteed success. The Scriptures make it very clear, however, that the authority does not reside in saying the right words, or even in the use of the name of Jesus. The experience of the seven sons of Sceva makes that abundantly clear. When they tried to use the name of Jesus as they had heard Paul do, they discovered the authority didn't reside in a magic formula or even in the name of Jesus. The power only backed up the authority when the person using the name was living and serving under the authority of the Lord Jesus Christ.

Jesus also stated this clearly in His Sermon on the Mount when He said, "Many will say to me on that day, 'Lord, Lord, did we not prophesy *in your name*, and *in your name* cast out demons and perform many miracles?'

Then I will tell them plainly, 'I never knew you. Away from me, you evildoers'" (Matthew 7:22, 23, italics added).

The effectiveness of the exercise of authority in the name of the Lord Jesus Christ depends on the faith of the believer and the degree to which the believer is living under the authority of God. We cannot expect to be effective in resisting the devil if we are not first in true submission to God. Peter confirms this when he says, "Humble yourselves, therefore, under God's mighty hand"; then we can "resist" this enemy who "prowls around like a roaring lion looking for someone to devour" (1 Peter 5:6-9).

CHAPTER SEVEN

THE CHRISTIAN DEFENSIVE

A WYCLIFFE BIBLE TRANSLATOR WRITES:

I went to the Amazon Jungle in 1963 in order to begin our ministry among the Apurina people.... So far as I know I was the first one to challenge Satan's dominion over this people, a total domination down through the centuries. My basic purpose in being there was to see if I could remove that people from Satan's house and take them to Jesus' house, if I could transfer them from the kingdom of darkness to the kingdom of light. But unfortunately, in spite of a Master of Theology degree and having read the Bible through several times, I was not aware of these truths [about spiritual warfare]. I got clobbered! I got it without mercy, until I had had enough. Satan wiped the floor with me. I didn't know how to defend myself—actually, I didn't really understand what was happening. You see, I was skeptical about the activity of the demons. Oh yes, I knew that Satan and the demons exist, because the Bible is clear and emphatic on that score, but I knew very little about how they operate and virtually nothing about the use of our weapons, whether for defense or offense. My theological background, both formal and informal, was strictly traditional. . . . My professors transmitted the idea that a servant of Christ was untouchable or exempt from demonic attack; that sort of thing wouldn't be a problem for us.[1]

But it is not only on the mission field that such attacks happen. A pastor called me to secure help with counseling a demonized person who had come to him. But in the course of our talking with each other, he told me there was a strange pall or spirit of heaviness in their services which they could not account for ever since they had gone to that church. Then they discovered that some people who had become involved in occult activity and who had refused the counsel of the church in relation to it had become hostile toward the church and had put curses on it with their occult powers. When the pastor and his elders claimed the power of the Cross against this curse and rededicated their building and grounds to the glory of God, they reported that the change of spirit in the service the next Sunday was "unbelievable."

Yes, Christians do come under demonic attack. The warnings in the New Testament about conflict with Satan and demons are all addressed to believers. This is a conflict in which we are involved whether we want to be or not. And the stakes in the battle are high—the glory of God. Failure on our part to be good soldiers (2 Timothy 2:4) will result in a poor witness to the world about the character of the God we serve. Our enemy is committed to making us ineffective in our personal lives and in our ministries for our Lord. He "prowls around like a roaring lion looking for someone to devour" (1 Peter 5:8). He knows that he has already been defeated at the Cross and that his time is limited (Revelation 12:12), but he uses every means he can to keep the believers on earth from believing that or at least from acting on it.

The Christian and Demons

One of the first questions to be raised in connection with the idea of demonic attacks on a Christian is whether such is even possible, and if so to what extent.

Only eternity will reveal the number of believers who have led unproductive, frustrated lives and of Christian workers who have been forced to forsake their ministries because of attacks of the enemy. This happens in spite of the fact that the New Testament warnings concerning demonic activity are all addressed to believers. Peter was writing to Christians when he said,

> Be self-controlled and alert. Your enemy the devil prowls around like a roaring lion looking for someone to devour. Resist him, standing firm in the faith, because you know that your brothers throughout the world are undergoing the same kind of sufferings. (1 Peter 5:8, 9)

How "resist" got changed to "ignore" in so many segments of the Church, I don't know. When it did, however, Satan and his forces gained a great strategic advantage.

I will not rehearse the various views on the extent to which a Christian may be affected by demons. This topic has been covered by many writers on spiritual warfare. (See especially C. Fred Dickason, *Demon Possession and the Christian*, Crossway, 1989.) I am among those, however, who believe that the use of the word "possession" to translate the expressions used in the Greek New Testament to indicate the relationship between demons and people is unfortunate, if not unwarranted. We obtained our English word *demon* by transliterating the Greek word *daimon*. We should have done the same thing with the Greek word *daimonizomai*—a verb form from the same Greek root. It would come into English as "demonize," and we could then speak of the degree to which a person could be demonized rather than being limited to the either-or options imposed by the possessed—not possessed view. My study and experience have convinced me that a Christian may be attacked by demons and may be affected mentally and sometimes physically at significant levels, but that this does not constitute possession or ownership. I recognize that these terms are defined differently by different people, but spiritual "possession" clearly implies ownership and would seem to include the control of one's eternal destiny. In either case it would be impossible to be owned and controlled by Satan and have a saving relationship with Christ at the same time. So if the question is, "Can a Christian be demon-possessed?" the answer is clearly no.

Reasons for Attacks on Christians

But a prior question to be asked is, Why would a demon want to attack a Christian if it knows that the Christ who lives in the believer makes that person more than a match for any demon (see Romans 8:35-37; 1 John 4:4)? The obvious answer is, to keep the Christian from believing and acting on that truth. But there are many other reasons for demons to focus on believers as well.

In talking about the fall of Satan, we indicated that his jealousy of us as the crown of God's creation may have played some role in his ongoing rebellion against God. Whether that is true or not, it is one good reason for him to hate us now. It may be helpful at this point to look at some other reasons for Satan's hatred of believers.

The most obvious of these is that we are created in the image of God. This links us with God in a unique way. Satan thought he had destroyed this link by getting Adam and Eve to follow his suggestion that disobeying God would somehow make them like God. The seeds of humanism were planted right there in the Garden of Eden. God, however, was not content to let that process go on unchallenged. He immediately provided a means of reconciliation through "the Lamb that was slain from the creation of the world" (Revelation 13:8) and He thus is our Maker both by creation and by re-creation. Peter tells us that "His divine power has given us everything we need for life and godliness through the knowledge of him who called us by his own glory and goodness." And through His own glory and goodness "he has given us his very great and precious promises, so that through them [we] may *participate in the divine nature* and escape the corruption in the world caused by evil desires" (2 Peter 1:3, 4, italics added). This participation in the "divine nature" is reason enough for Satan to be jealous of us.

We have noted in Ephesians 1 Paul's use of the figure of adoption to speak of our relationship with the Lord. This also has to infuriate Satan. The idea that we have left his family and been adopted into God's family is an obvious affront to him. By virtue of that adoption, we became God's heirs. Paul makes this very explicit in Romans 8:17, and he also specifically prays that the Ephesian Christians would know God's "glorious inheritance in the saints" (Ephesians 1:18). While that has implications for the next life, it certainly has significant implications for this life as well. Satan would love to keep us ignorant of what it means to be heirs of God.

In our role as God's children and His heirs, we are His primary representatives here on earth. If Satan can get us to live our lives at a level that is less than to the glory of God, he can keep us from fulfilling the purpose for which we were created and re-created. A Christian who does not know how to appropriate the power of God to overcome the attacks of the enemy is certainly not living life to the glory of God. So Satan is quite content simply to cause Christians to live spiritually ineffective lives. Not to recognize this as part of the spiritual encounter is to miss a primary tactic of the enemy. Satan is not threatened by religious activity, but he is threatened and angered by the demonstration of the power of God to live victorious, godly lives.

There is more reason for Satan to hate us, however. Not only has God made us in His image, not only has He given us "everything we need for life and godliness," He has commissioned us with His authority to invade the territory of the enemy and reclaim it for the Lord. Even a godly life lived in isolation from the world is not the threat to Satan that active, powerful ministry is. So a self-centered pursuit of holiness may even be encouraged so long as one does not become motivated to evangelize the unreached peoples of the world.

The ultimate test of any spiritual revival is whether or not it becomes missionary. Satan may not be able to stop a revival in a local church, but if he can keep it there and get the people to focus on their own holiness, he can at least prevent God's ultimate purpose from being realized.

Since believers are the spiritually commissioned and empowered army of God, Satan must seek to neutralize them at any cost. This has many implications, but we note at this point only that there is ample reason for Satan to be on the attack against Christians, especially those who are pressing the spiritual battle on the front lines.

The Extent of Demonic Control

Assuming adequate motivation for attack, and given the Biblical warnings to be prepared for attack, we may then ask to what extent demons can influence or otherwise affect Christians.

We need to begin this discussion with a recognition that the Bible does not make any clear, didactic statement on this subject. Nowhere does it say a believer cannot have an evil spirit in him, and nowhere does it say he can. This absence of clear teaching can be frustrating, but it is not without precedent in other key areas of doctrine. There is no didactic passage, for example, from which to teach the doctrine of the Trinity per se. In such cases one has to take what is taught in various Scriptures that relates to the subject, consider what the Church has taught down through the centuries, and evaluate present experience in the light of the first two.

I do not propose to review the treatment of this question which Fred Dickason has done so well in his book *Demon Possession and the Christian.* A few thoughts on the topic will help to provide a setting for the rest of our discussion, however.

In the absence of categorical statements on the subject, we revert to reason as one of the approaches to the questions raised. This leads us to the argument that since my body is the temple of the Holy Spirit, an evil spirit cannot also be in my body. This thinking is based on the law that two objects cannot occupy the same space at the same time. The fallacy with the argument is that spirits do not occupy space, nor is being Spirit-filled a matter of space. It is rather a matter of the degree to which all of my life is lived under the guidance which comes from God through the ministry of "the Spirit of wisdom and revelation" (Ephesians 1:17). Furthermore, if God and an evil spirit cannot be at the same place at the same time, then, given the omnipresence of God, demons cannot be anywhere.

The point to be made is that logic based on physical analogies fails us when we are dealing with the spirit world. The way in which the spirit world and our physical bodies interact is also an area of study which baffles the scientists. They, of course, do not usually speak of spirits, but they do recognize a nonmaterial part of a person that seems to run the physical part of the person. There is talk, for example, about mind and brain and how they interact. Sir John Eccles, in his book *The Neurophysiological Basis of the Mind*,[2] says, "In this discussion of the functioning of the brain, it has initially been regarded as a 'machine' operating according to the laws of physics and chemistry." He goes on to express the frustrations of the scientists, however, when he says, "It would appear that it [the brain] is the sort of machine a 'ghost' could operate, if by ghost we mean in the first place an 'agent' whose action has escaped detection even by the most delicate physical instruments."[3] The human brain is clearly part of the physical body, and it will remain with the body after death. It is, however, the control room for all the rest of the body, and whoever controls it controls the body.

The issue at hand is the degree to which I control it by my own psyche, the Holy Spirit controls it through my submission to him, or a demon controls it through the lies which he deceives me into believing. We generally understand that the more healthy I am in my thinking, the more healthy will be the expressions of my life through my body. This is why we are admonished by Solomon, "Above all else, guard your heart, for it is the wellspring of life" (Proverbs 4:23).

If we are believers, the Holy Spirit becomes a significant part of our lives to the extent that we do not "grieve" Him (Ephesians 4:30). This influence may range from help with the most basic processes of life to the supernatural gifting exhibited by Jonathan Goforth in China. Goforth's command of the Chinese language was such that the Chinese did not like to have him try to preach in their language. They preferred that he use an interpreter. Then one night God gave him the gift of speaking Chinese, and that night the people did not want him to stop preaching. The Holy Spirit was sending stimuli into Goforth's brain that were clearly not "natural." The Holy Spirit, can do that, and that gift continued throughout his life.[4]

Evil spirits also have access to our brains. They can tempt us by introducing thoughts into our minds. Satan even did that with Jesus. Demons went much further than that with the Gadarene demoniac. There is no reason to believe that demons bypass the brain in such cases. So the issue is not whether a demon is in my body causing some undesirable activity, but whether it has access to my mind through my failure to use my defenses against it.

We are talking about the relationship between my spirit, the Holy Spirit, and an evil spirit. That is not a spatial matter. It is a spiritual one, and the location of the demon—inside or outside—is not the real issue. The issue is, to whom do I yield control?

When I become a believer, the Holy Spirit comes to live in me. A demon can never force Him to leave (1 John 4:4). As I "keep in step with the Spirit" (Galatians 5:25), walking in faith and obedience, I do not need to fear demonic invasion. That is not to say I do not need to be prepared for the enemy's attacks, but it is to say that I do not need to live in fear. If, however, I do not pursue the truth and do not walk in obedience, I may give the enemy ground for a successful attack.

This may be likened to a country which has an enemy that would like to overthrow the government and transfer control to a rebel group. The enemy does not have the resources to launch a frontal attack; so they set up a base camp from which they conduct guerrilla raids into the country. This does not drive the government out, but it does keep the country on edge and forces it to marshal many more resources than usual in order to protect itself against the guerrilla attacks.

As with the guerrilla forces, the demons are not able to overthrow the spiritual government of one's life if that is in the hands of the Holy Spirit. But if we are giving ground to the enemy through believing his deceptions or through unconfessed sin, we should not be surprised if the enemy takes advantage of that opportunity to step up his level of attack. If the relationship between believers and demons is seen in this light, the relationship will fall along a spectrum running from the level of victory experienced by Jesus Himself at one end and an entrenched enemy that is camping on ground which has not been brought under the rule of truth and the Lordship of Christ at the other. Just as there are degrees of relationship to the Holy Spirit ranging from the "worldly" Christian of 1 Corinthians 3 to the mature, fruitful servant of Christ, so there are degrees of relationship to Satan and demons.

The good news in all of this is that we have the truth about the defeat of this enemy and the triumph of our Lord, and when we walk in that truth, the truth will set us free (John 8:32). I have no basis for assuming that my protection is automatic regardless of how I handle that truth, but I have every reason to believe that the sovereign God who is the source of the truth can never fail.

CHAPTER EIGHT

ATTACKS IN THE PHYSICAL REALM

SPIRITUAL WARFARE, LIKE ALMOST any other kind of war, has an offensive and a defensive dimension to it. The two are not mutually exclusive. They are, in fact, often closely related. It would seem only reasonable that Satan would be especially concerned with any believer who is committed to carrying out God's purposes on earth and that the more aggressive one became on the offensive side, the stronger the counterattacks. This would be especially true of those who are seeking to raise up a witness for the Lord among a group of people who have known only the rule of the "god of this age [or world]" (2 Corinthians 4:4). The more active one becomes in this type of ministry and the more effective one is in declaring and demonstrating the glory of God and in challenging the power of Satan, the more demonic opposition one may expect. So attacks on the defensive level may be the result of encounters on the offensive level. It may be helpful, however, to look at them separately.

The problem often is that even Christian workers reflect the prevailing worldview and do not consider demonic attack as a possible cause of personal problems being faced, or perhaps they are not aware of the nature of such attacks. As a result they do not take effective action against the attackers.

With this as background, we will look at some of the types of encounter which can be categorized as demonic attacks on the Christian. Many of the illustrations come from missionary experiences, partly because this is the area of my special interest and partly as a basis for Christians at home to understand better how to pray for missionaries.

Attacks Involving the Physical Body

It is clear from Scripture that demons have the ability to attack the human body in various ways, especially through disease (Matthew 9:32, 33; Luke 13:16; 2 Corinthians 12:7; etc.). Job is a classic example of this, and we meet it a number of times in the ministry of Jesus as well. This is not a phenomenon limited to the time of Jesus, however, nor is it limited to the non-Christian world. Anyone who has not learned to use the spiritual armor and weapons effectively is open to such attack.

For example, a young lady missionary who had been teaching in Colombia, South America, was forced to come home because she became so physically debilitated that she couldn't function normally. After two years of going from doctor to doctor and clinic to clinic without any help, she became so discouraged that she decided to give up even trying to be a Christian. Although she had been in Satan's territory, where demonic activity was known to be very prevalent, no one had seriously suggested that the cause of her problem might be demonic. But on the morning she decided to put her Bible on the shelf, the Lord said to her, "Why don't you fast and pray and cast them out?" She knew very little about dealing with demons, but she decided that she had nothing to lose but her problem; so she decided to try.

Her first attempts at prayer were futile. No words would come out. She therefore decided to write a basic command against demons on a card and read it every thirty minutes during the day. After reading it the first time, she was able to pray; and she went through the day reading her Bible, praying, and reading her command to the demons every thirty minutes. By the end of the day she was a new person. She said, "The change was so great, I could hardly take it [in]." Yet, it was a week before she could accept the fact that her healing was real and permanent. She has since that time lived a productive Christian life.[1]

I am not suggesting that all physical problems are demonic, nor that the method the young lady used is the model everyone should employ in resisting the enemy. I would suggest, however, that more physical problems have a demonic involvement than we have recognized. And as a result Satan wins another round in the spiritual war by taking a Christian soldier out of the conflict.

A pastor in one of my classes was developing the symptoms of a crippling disease. He had been through all of the standard medical tests, but the doctor said he could find no scientific confirmation that he actually had the disease. A tip-off that this might be more than a medical problem came in the form of a voice that told him every time he saw someone in a wheelchair, "Five years from now, that's you." It is now five years later, and the pastor is carrying on a full ministry with no signs of the disease. His route to freedom was in taking back the ground the demons claimed in the form of broken family relationships. When that was done, their power was gone and he was free.

In a village in Sierra Leone, where I served, early missionaries were given "the devil's hill" on which to build the mission house. No one took the danger of this seriously because "demons couldn't do anything to Christians." When I was on the field I had a nonfunctional theology about such things, but I vividly remember watching the family living in that house go through attacks of physical disease which eventually took them off the field. A recent occupant of that house told me that until two years ago people who came to visit would become ill when they arrived but would lose the symptoms as they left the village. Why the change? Two years ago they finally cleansed the hill in a power encounter. Since that time there have been no more physical attacks. God alone knows how many of His servants have been taken out of the battle because they did not recognize this device of the enemy.

Attacks Involving the Appetites

Attacks are not limited, however, to disease. They may come in the area of the physical appetites. W. L. McLeod tells of a woman who came to him plagued with a compulsive eating disorder. For four years she had been battling something in her which compelled her to literally run to food, stuff it into her mouth, vomit it, and do it all over again. She and her husband reported that their food bill was "enormous." A little probing revealed that she was also involved in four different kinds of occult activity. When she saw what the Scriptures have to say about such activity, she renounced her participation as sin, then claimed freedom from the demons causing the compulsive behavior, and she was set free.[2]

There can be little doubt these days that Satan and his army of demons are making an all-out attack on Christian workers in the area of sexual appetites, and it seems that no one is immune from this. The world provides plenty of stimuli in the wrong direction on this subject, and the devil is glad to take full advantage of the situation. Add to this equation the fact that few Christians are aware of the spiritual dimensions to this battle. Many think it is just a matter of the flesh and that they have that area of their lives under control. I had a ministry colleague say to me when I confronted him about an affair he had been carrying on with another man's wife, "I never thought I could be tempted in this area." All too many have let down their guard because they have become overconfident and thus vulnerable.

A seasoned missionary came to me after one of my classes to seek help. He told me that perverted sexual thoughts would come into his mind almost every time he tried to pray. He was too embarrassed to talk with anyone about it, so he just tried to bear it as "his cross." I asked him if those thoughts came from God. Obviously they didn't. Then I asked if they were his thoughts—if he liked them and dreamed them up. He said that, on the contrary, he hated them. "Then where do you think they come from?" I asked. He had never considered that these thoughts might be coming from an enemy. I told him how to reject them, refuse to own them, or let them control him, and to resist the spirit sending them on the basis of his position in Christ. He came back about a year later and stopped by my office to say, "I just want to thank you for what you taught me last year. I thought that you might pray over me, cast out a demon, and make my problem go away, but I'm glad it didn't work that way. I have learned so much this year. It has changed my life, my marriage, my family, and I am going back to the field with a whole new attitude toward my ministry."

At this point someone is certain to accuse me of finding a demon behind every human problem or to say, "Don't you find it even more unsettling to a person to suggest that they may have a demonic problem?" On the

contrary, the suggestion that there is something funda-
mentally wrong with them for having such a problem is
what is unsettling, and to discover that there is something or someone outside themselves causing the situation is a great relief. That is not to say that personal
responsibility does not need to be faced. It always does.
But to ignore an unscrupulous enemy who always seeks
to take advantage of a difficult situation by making it
worse and to fail to appropriate the victory of Christ is
folly.

We know that we have to contend with the flesh.
What we have failed to recognize is that the devil and his
demons take advantage of the flesh to put us under pressure which we cannot handle through normal Christian
disciplines. It takes the skillful use of spiritual weapons
to destroy such strongholds of the enemy. Satan has convinced many Christian leaders they are not subject to
temptation in the sexual area. Even where there has
been a family history of weakness in this area, some fail
to recognize the activity of the enemy, and so we have
seen some tragic consequences both for the persons
involved and for the cause of Christ.

Attacks Involving Physical Objects

Demons can affect not only the human body, but also
physical objects. We need to recognize the clear distinc-
tion which the Scriptures make between the object as
such and the demon behind the object. This is seen most
clearly in the passages which deal with idolatry. One set
of passages treats the idols with utter contempt because
in their own identity, as pieces of wood, metal, or stone,
the idols have absolutely no power. Jeremiah 10:3-5 is an
example of such passages—passages which should be
read with sarcasm:

For the customs of the peoples are worthless;
   they cut a tree out of the forest,
and a craftsman shapes it with his chisel.
   They adorn it with silver and gold;
they fasten it with hammer and nails
   so it will not totter.
Like a scarecrow in a melon patch,
   their idols cannot speak;
they must be carried
   because they cannot walk.
Do not fear them; they can do no harm
   nor can they do any good.

See Psalm 115:4-8; Isaiah 40:18-20; 41:7, 21-24; 44:9-20; Jeremiah 10:14, 15 for other examples of this type of passage.

Another set of passages, however, clearly relate idols to demons. See, for example, Leviticus 17:7 ("goat idols"=demons); Deuteronomy 32:17; 2 Chronicles 11:15 ("goat and calf idols"=demons); Psalm 106:37; Revelation 9:20. This is made explicit in 1 Corinthians 10:19-21 where Paul says,

Do I mean then that a sacrifice offered to an idol is anything, or that an idol is anything? No, but the sacrifices of pagans are offered to demons, not to God, and I do not want you to be participants with demons.

When objects are made for occult purposes, or when people look to an object with the anticipation that it has power, demons will meet their expectation quite apart from any qualities inherent in the object itself. Or, in other cases, a person engaging in occult practices may invite demons to empower an object, and in this way the demons may become associated with that object. The practice of ignoring such demonic power or of assuming that demons cannot harm a Christian has led to many problems for missionaries.

For example, a young lady shared the following story with me, prefaced by the comment, "It is good to have someone to talk with about this who won't think I'm crazy." She was studying French in preparation for service in Africa. She was by nature a very energetic, outgoing person; but she had become very depressed and was having difficulty sleeping and studying. After struggling with this for awhile, a missionary with whom she had become acquainted asked her where she was staying. Upon examining her room, they discovered that the previous occupant had placed many occult objects in the room. Apparently some of the spirits associated with those objects had attached themselves to the room and its furnishings. They prayed, commanding the spirits to leave, and that night the new missionary slept normally and was able to continue her language study.

A missionary in the Philippines had moved into a mission home previously occupied by a family that had had unusual problems with their five-year-old son— problems which seemed to occur only while the boy was at home. There was a large tree in the front yard under which the new missionary put a sandbox for their son to play in. The local pastor warned the missionary that an evil spirit was known to live in that tree and that it was therefore not a good place to put the sandbox. The missionary said, "We felt that even if that were true, it wouldn't bother us because we were believers."

One day the missionaries heard their son screaming and crying. The wife ran out to find their thirty-five-pound boy trying to choke their seventy-five-pound German shepherd. The boy was properly scolded and admonished about treating the dog in that way, and the incident was dismissed. About three days later the same thing happened. As they began to discipline their son he said, "But, Mommy, I don't want to kill my doggy; something made me do it." Further questioning revealed that something had come down from the tree, taken his hands, and forced him to choke the dog. The missionary began taking the demon's presence seriously, and the next time this happened he and his wife commanded the demon in the name of Jesus to leave and asked God to put a hedge of protection around them. That solved their problem.

The point is, Satan will use any avenue he can to prevent missionaries (or any Christian workers) from carrying on their ministries. And when the local people see that the missionaries do not know how to handle an encounter which they clearly perceive to be demonic, the cause of the gospel is hindered, to say the least. In the minds of the people, when the missionary fails to win in a power encounter, the power of the demon is assumed to be greater than the power of the Christ the missionary serves. A successful meeting of such a challenge, however, is powerful witness to the gospel.

Otto Koning, a missionary to New Guinea, tells of going to a village for the first time to hold services there. The people had built a special shelter for the meeting, and it was packed to the palm-frond walls with curious people. But conducting a service was another matter. The babies cried, the dogs outside barked, and to top it off a very large pig came crashing through the wall of the shelter, causing pandemonium among the people. Koning finally gave up in defeat and headed for home.

He was understandably not too eager to return to the village, but he had promised he would. Fortunately he had also been learning about spiritual warfare and the reality of demonic interference toward attempts to bring the gospel to a new village. So he began to wonder if demons might have been behind the disturbance in the village and if they could be bound before he went there. It was worth a try; so he commanded the demons not to use the animals to disturb the service. This time even the babies didn't seem to cry as much, and the animals stayed at the other end of the village. The result was that the gospel was heard and people came to Christ.

The typical Western mind will attribute this to coincidence, but anyone who has been in the battle has no difficulty understanding the reality of the power of demons to use animals or other objects in the physical world to hinder the work of God and of God's servants. Understanding this is the first step in claiming victory over it.

CHAPTER NINE

ATTACKS IN THE SPIRITUAL REALM

IT IS NOT ONLY in the physical realm that believers may expect attack from the enemy. The principal objective of Satan, as we have already noted, is to render God's servants spiritually ineffective. There is a sense in which all spiritual warfare is a matter of spiritual effectiveness or ineffectiveness. At the root of this matter is the maturity level of our personal and corporate Christian lives. It is imperative that we be aware of the tactics Satan uses to disrupt our lives in this area.

One of his very productive tactics has been promoting the move away from a functional belief in demons and demon-caused problems in this world to the assumption that there is a scientific explanation for all such phenomena. With that drift there often seems to be a corresponding tendency to question the supernatural activity of God as well. Spirit causation, whether evil spirits or the Holy Spirit, is too often questioned. His ultimate aim is always to get us to doubt the character of God and to reject His authority in our lives. This often manifests itself in a questioning of the authority of God's Word. When that authority is gone, not far behind is the drift to universalism—a doctrine which is the mortal enemy of world evangelization.

There are, however, other ways of undermining the authority of God's Word. Friends of mine who come from solid evangelical stock and who had a real heart for God became involved in a group where spiritual gifts were apparently operating. At first the prophecies were in harmony with the Scriptures, and it was an exhilarating experience to see this type of power. Gradually the words began to be more special and not according to the usual understanding of Biblical truth. By this time, however, they had come to trust the prophecies to such an extent that they were afraid to question them. Eventually at least five homes were broken by divorces ordered "by the spirit," and when confronted about this on the basis of Scripture the people were unwilling to listen. In the guise of super-spirituality, the authority of the Word of God had been undermined. It is obvious, however, that the spirit giving the instructions was not the Holy Spirit.

This seems to be a similar situation to the one which caused Paul to write to the Corinthians, "I am afraid that just as Eve was deceived by the serpent's cunning, your minds may somehow be led astray from your sincere and pure devotion to Christ" (2 Corinthians 11:3).

Not only does this kind of deception affect the individuals involved, but if those who are ready to accept almost anything supernatural as being from God end up on the same ministry team as those who allow for no demonstration of power in the form of spiritual gifts or power encounters, the ministry greatly suffers. I have encountered such situations in my travels and have heard of many more.

Satan's deception does not need to be as dramatic as counterfeit spiritual gifts, however. He has become expert at selling believers wrong views about God and therefore wrong views about themselves.

I have learned not to take anything for granted in this area. Most Christians who come for help know the right answers at the theological level, but even people in full-time ministry may be the victims of wrong beliefs about God at the functional level. I have heard some shocking things from the mouths of people in Christian service. The problem often is that we do not maintain a climate in the Church where people dare to be honest. As a result, they keep their true thoughts hidden and do not deal with the real problem. Neil Anderson's two books referred to earlier deal most insightfully with this problem.

There are, of course, many areas of spiritual life where we may become vulnerable. But most of them will be cared for if we begin with a commitment to saying the truth about everything in our lives, to being honest about our emotions and thoughts, and to living as the new persons we become when we are "in Christ."

Attacks on the Mind

Related to, and indeed lying behind all of the areas of encounter we have discussed, is the human psyche and especially the mind. This is the real battleground in most instances. It is probably never correct to say, "The Devil made me do it." He may have started the process, just as he did with Eve, but we are responsible for what we do with what he puts in our minds. Failure to recognize the source of the thought and to reject it is the problem. John Newport says:

Fallen angels cannot act directly upon the will, but they can and do act upon the imaginations, thoughts, emotions and desires. Where they find a passion alive and active in us, they can play upon these passions and fantasies and so intensify the passion. Evidently they can also inject fantasies and feelings which have no ground in our own character and experience.[1]

This relates to the frequently asked question, "How can you tell whether it is a demon or just the flesh?" My answer to that question is that it is almost always both, at least to some extent. A demon charged with harassing me would be a fool to see me having an emotional or mental problem and not try to complicate it. It is true that I am "lured and enticed," as the RSV puts it, "by [my] own desire" (James 1:14). The flesh is always involved. But Satan is not so foolish as not to take advantage of the struggle going on within me. So I need to be ready to deal with my part of it, but I also need to be ready to deal with the enemy.

A tactic Satan gets a great deal of mileage from is to put a thought into our mind and then accuse us for having it. He says, "You're supposed to be such a good Christian, but in view of what you're thinking there must be something really wrong with you." Many people, even missionaries or evangelists or pastors, live with a pervasive sense of guilt and unworthiness simply because they don't recognize this tactic of the enemy. This was in reality the problem of the "seasoned missionary" with the perverted sexual thoughts referred to in Chapter 8.

A related tactic is to trigger an emotional reaction and then use the same accusation approach. Satan has many people convinced that they are what they feel— whether those feelings be "good" or "bad." Feelings are not unimportant. They are a very real part of our lives, but they are not the test of truth or of spirituality. This is why Christian meditation is so important. Meditating on the Word of God day and night builds a Biblical filter in the mind by which that which is contrary to the truth is kept out. So when the enemy tries to accuse us for a thought he planted in our mind, we can say, "I recognize where that thought came from, and since it is not from God I reject it. I refuse to be controlled by it." My wife would tell you that since I have learned to do this I am much easier to live with. I am not claiming perfection, but I am learning and growing.

One night I went to bed discouraged. A particular situation was going over and over in my mind. That is a bit unusual for me. I usually go to sleep before I go to bed rather than not going to sleep after I go to bed. (I "preach" that God is in the business of encouraging us; Satan is in the business of discouraging us. The key word is *courage*, the attitude with which I am to face the circumstances of life.) In any case, the Lord said to me that night, "Why don't you practice what you preach?" And I said, "Right, Lord. I teach that discouragement is always from the devil. So I am sinning if I allow discouragement to control me. Forgive me. I resist whatever spirit is putting me under this pressure, and I choose to think Your thoughts." With that I began meditating on a Psalm, but before I got far, I was asleep.

This truth has special application to interpersonal relations. Again, I do not wish to suggest that there is a simplistic answer to all human relationships, but I believe that many church conflicts and missionary incompatibilities involve more than just personality conflicts.

To help my wife and me understand this, I think the Lord allowed us to go through such an experience a few years ago. We have a very romantic story about how the Lord brought us together after the untimely deaths of our first mates, and many people have spoken to us about how our relationship has ministered to them. I should add that this was not a case of "living happily ever after"; we have had to work at our relationship. But I say this as background to the fact that we suddenly began to have compulsively critical attitudes toward each other. There was no big issue involved—not something we needed to sit down and work out; just a compulsively critical attitude. Satan was getting great mileage from it, because we could no longer function effectively as a ministry team.

Finally the Lord led us separately to identify what was going on. We were under enemy attack. When I recognized that, I again said, "Lord, I know this is not from You. Forgive me for ever allowing it to control me. And I command the spirit doing this to leave." Immediately it was gone. My wife did the same thing, still with no communication between us, and we were back to normal—not to perfection, just to normal. A level of compulsion is frequently an evidence of demonic involvement, but it is not often recognized.

I know of missionary situations where on certain stations there seems to be an unusual amount of this type of tension. Missionaries will say something like, "It seems that no matter who is stationed there, they can't get along." Seldom, however, is demonic power considered as a contributing cause.

Attacks Based on Occult Connections

Demonic activity in Christians may be rooted in a variety of causes. The common assumption that Christians are somehow immune from such attacks, however, has often caused us to overlook basic problems like, for example, involvement in innocent-looking but nevertheless occult practices.

A missionary in Africa was experiencing "physical and nervous weakness" which could not be diagnosed or successfully treated either on the field or after she returned to Canada. While in Africa she had been involved in one unique activity which brought her a good bit of satisfaction. She had discovered that she could locate sites for new wells by dowsing or water-witching. She assumed that since a good end was being served, the dowsing was all right. Through a book she was reading, however, she learned that dowsing had occult connections. So, as her husband tells the story,

> . . . to check it out she took a rod out to a place where she knew it would work. When it began "pumping" she said, "If this is a gift of God I accept it, but if it is of Satan, I reject it." Promptly [the wand] stood still. . . . She repented and asked God to forgive and cleanse and heal her of its evil effects. The physical weakness and nervous condition disappeared, and she returned to Africa with good health for further service.[2]

Attacks Based on Curses

Curses from practitioners of the black arts may also be involved. Missionaries on furlough from their service in South America, for example, were greatly disturbed when their teenaged son and daughter grew rebellious and became involved in conduct which led to the son being arrested by the police for theft. While talking with the pastor of one of their supporting churches, they began to put some things together that they had overlooked earlier.

On the field they had been conducting Bible studies for children, and the children of the local witch doctor were attending. They had been coached by their father to disrupt the class, and the missionary finally had to forbid them to come. As a result the witch doctor came and placed a curse on the missionary's family. The missionaries had seen him out in the street going through his incantations, but they assumed no harm could come to them because they were Christians. Looking back on all that, however, they began to take the curse seriously. They renounced it in Jesus' name and commanded any demons enforcing the curse to go to the Cross to make their claim. The children's rebelliousness immediately disappeared, and the family was able to return to the field, with the son and daughter actively participating in the ministry along with their parents.[3]

Attacks Based on Personal Sin

The cause of enemy attacks may be personal sin one has tried to hide. Our churches, unfortunately, have often not encouraged honesty when it comes to certain kinds of sin. We are, rather, taught by the example of others to wear a mask when we come to church—a mask which says, "everything in my life is just fine." Behind the mask may be a desperately hurting person. But we play our game, the basic rule of which is: "If you don't remove my mask, I won't remove yours."

The sin which probably does more damage than any other is unforgiveness and all the attitudes which surround it. For example, a missionary couple had to come home because the husband had become so depressed he simply could not function. Two years of psychiatric treatment produced no improvement. When they came to my friend for counsel, the wife had to do all of the talking at first. The Lord led the counselor to the conclusion that resentments were involved. Although this was stoutly denied initially, the missionary was sent away to make a list of any persons against whom he held resentments. The next day he returned with a long list. They worked through these one at a time, and he agreed to follow up any that needed personal confession and reconciliation.

At this point the demons behind this problem surfaced and were cast out, and the missionary expressed a deep, settled peace. When the couple came back the next day, he was obviously a different person. Rather than anticipating a forced retirement in the States, they were ready to resume their ministry on the field, a step they have subsequently taken.

To choose not to forgive is to choose to allow someone other than the Lord to control our life. It is to choose to be a victim when Christ wants to set us free. It is also to give ground to the enemy so he can set up a guerrilla base from which to operate in our lives (Ephesians 4:26, 27).

Forgiveness is a choice we make based on the clear teaching of Scripture that we are to forgive from our hearts (Matthew 6:14, 15; 18:35; Ephesians 4:32) and on the logic that the bitterness of unforgiveness does much more harm to the one who holds the bitterness than to the one they refuse to forgive.

One of the big problems for most people with forgiveness is what to do with the hurt. We cannot pretend that the hurt is not there. It exists, and it will not go away by wishing. The choice we have is whether we are going to go on allowing that hurt to control our lives. Forgiveness says, "I will accept the hurt as part of the price of forgiving, and I will trust the Lord to give me the grace needed to cope with it." It is often amazing what God does for us when we choose to do things His way. Many people want to say, "God, take the hurt away, and I will forgive." But God says, "You forgive, and I will deal with the hurt."

Satan will try to tell you that because you have decided to forgive but can still feel the hurt at times, you have not really forgiven. That is another of his lies.

Our memory systems are so made up that emotions often go with memory. I can remember, for example, a time when I had my wife, my four children, and my mother-in-law in the car on our way to Cleveland, Ohio. We came to a major highway from a side road on which we were traveling, but the stop sign was partially hidden by a tree. When I saw it and put on the brakes, I discovered there was sand on the road, and I literally slid right across the highway. When I think what could have happened if a semitrailer rig had been passing that intersection at the same instant, it literally gives me goose bumps. Does that mean I am in danger now? Not at all. Similarly, the memory of some past sin or abuse may trigger an emotion, but that does not mean I am under the control of that emotion. At such a time we need to say something along the lines of what I believe Clara Barton once said about something out of her past: "I distinctly remember forgetting that." We can simply renew our decision to forgive and get on with life in the strength of the Lord.

Other key areas that often need to be worked through are rebellion against authority, pride or self-centeredness, and fleshly sin. Such things always need to be faced honestly in the life of a believer, whether there is evidence of demonic activity or not. Regardless, it is safe to assume that Satan will always take advantage of the person who leaves the door open to him through such sins.

Attacks Based on Ancestral Sin

There is one other basis for demonic attack which needs to be identified. It is one which every experienced counselor has encountered again and again. Fred Dickason says that a majority of the persons to whom he has ministered had some measure of bondage due to ancestral sin.[4]

When God said that the sins of the fathers are visited on the children to the third and fourth generation (Exodus 20:5), He also said that He visits blessing on the children of those who love Him and keep His commandments (20:6). This is operative first on the generational level. One generation lives with the effects of the good or the bad done by the previous generation. That this has application at the personal level is readily accepted in the physical realm. A child born to parents who have defiled their bodies with drugs may come into the world with a chemical dependency on drugs for which the child has no responsibility whatever. He is the victim of the sins of the parents.

Nearly every counselor has also seen children who are the victims of the sins of the parents in the emotional area through all kinds of abuse, and the well-known fact is that abused children tend to become abusive parents if the consequences of that abuse are not healed in their own lives.

The same principle applies in the spiritual area. Demons claim that if a parent was giving them ground through unconfessed sin in his or her life, they have the right to harass the offspring of that person. This does not make the child guilty of the sins of the parents; everyone is responsible for his or her own sins. But the consequences of sin are still present and must be dealt with. This can be done by a simple act of faith in the provisions of the Cross to deal with sin. Renunciation of the sins of parents and ancestors should be a standard part of the conversion/discipleship process. In a Christian home the renunciation should be made once, and then the emphasis should be on the promise of blessing "to thousands who love me and keep my commandments" (Exodus 20:6).

Dean Hochstetler, Mennonite layman who has been officially ordained by his church for deliverance ministry, has for many years been helping people with areas of demonic bondage in their lives. One day a man who had come to his place of business began to tell him of some strange behavior by the man's wife. She would buy expensive items, charge them, and then burn the bills; as a result they were constantly plagued with bad debts. Sometimes she would even steal items. Money was not the problem. There was enough available to purchase what they needed.

Dean suggested that they come to his house to talk further about the problem. In the conversation it came to light that the woman's mother had practiced magical healing, a practice called "powwowing" in that area of northern Indiana. This, of course, is an occult practice and opens the doors to demonic activity. The woman renounced this activity as sin and claimed the canceling of ground given by her mother through such practices; the demons harassing her were commanded to leave.

About two weeks later the couple came back, and the wife said, "Why couldn't I have known this fifty years ago? Why have I had to live with this all my life?" The husband said that the change was like having a new wife. In the Early Church, this would have been handled as part of the conversion-baptism process. It is to our detriment that we have abandoned the practice of having every baptismal candidate renounce the devil and all of his works.

I am not suggesting that all problems are demonic. I am suggesting that demonic activity is a component in more problems than we have been ready to recognize and deal with. The problems will nearly always have a basis in human experience, but Satan takes advantage of those experiences to intensify them and make them seem unsolvable. The assumption that believers have automatic protection from demons has been proved wrong again and again, and every defeat has meant another battle in this warfare won by the enemy.

Spiritual warfare, then, does not begin when we demonstrate power on behalf of others. It begins with demonstrating power to meet the problems in our own lives. Many people never get to the point of being able to help others precisely because they do not win the first encounter or, having gone into ministry anyhow, they do not know how to resist the enemy's attacks. The attempt to find a safe place where the enemy does not have to be confronted face-to-face is in reality surrender to the enemy and forfeiting the battle to him.

Winning in spiritual warfare on the personal level is a necessary first step toward winning at the ministry level, and it is to that type of encounter that we turn next.

CHAPTER TEN

THE CHRISTIAN OFFENSIVE

The Need for Spiritual Offensive

The old athletic adage "A good defense is the best offense" may here be turned around to read, "A good offense is the best defense." It is all too easy to develop a defensive posture toward our spiritual enemy with an emphasis only on stopping his attacks. That may in the long run ascribe far more power to him than he deserves. Our commission is not just to repel the attacks of the enemy, but to invade his territory, liberate those he has held captive, and bring them into the freedom of God's Kingdom. We, like Paul, are sent into the world "to open their eyes and turn them from darkness to light, and from the power of Satan to God, so that they may receive forgiveness of sins and a place among those who are sanctified by faith in [Christ]" (Acts 26:18).

As soldiers in this spiritual battle, we have confidence that the decisive victory was won at the Cross and that it is only a matter of time before the enemy is completely vanquished. The problem is that the Church often does not act in accordance with that fact. Instead of obeying their commission by moving out against the enemy, Christians are trying to have as little to do with the battle as possible.

The Old Testament pictures a similar situation. The children of Israel had been told by God that He was giving them the land of Canaan. He promised He would send His angel ahead of them to drive out the enemy. He demonstrated His ability to do this by showing His power over all the gods of Egypt, by bringing them out of captivity there, and by giving them victory over every conceivable kind of enemy—human and natural—on their trek to Mount Sinai. Israel, however, chose all too often to focus on the negatives: the strength of the enemies they met, the hardships along the way ·in the wilderness, and the evil report of the ten spies who focused on the walled cities and the giants rather than the power of God. As a result they spent thirty-eight years unnecessarily wandering in the wilderness.

We used to sing a chorus which said, "My Lord knows the way through the wilderness; all I have to do is follow." That idea is all right if we have in mind the wilderness between the Land of Goshen in Egypt and Kadesh Barnea. But if we are talking about the wilderness from Kadesh Barnea to Shittim, the idea is all wrong. Israel should not have been in that wilderness fighting meaningless battles. They should have entered the Promised Land at Kadesh Barnea and marched into Canaan to claim their inheritance. The wilderness wanderings are an illustration of spiritual mediocrity—a wilderness in which much, if not most, of the Western Church is found today.

There is a sense in which it is easier to be in the wilderness than in Canaan. In the wilderness they had manna to eat, their clothes and shoes didn't wear out, and they had little more to do than to follow the pillar of cloud when it moved. In Canaan there were battles to be fought, enemies to be driven out, farms to be made, and a whole new way of life to be learned. The Israelites may well have asked, "Who needs that?"

Likewise, today many are quite content to go to church on Sunday to collect their spiritual manna, but they are not really interested in doing their own farming. They are glad somebody is doing something about overseas heathen and inner cities at home, but who needs the kinds of problems associated with that type of ministry? They say, "This business of demons can do nothing but complicate one's life, so it is best to have as little to do with them as possible. Somebody needs to deal with those kinds of problems, but not me."

But the conquest of Canaan has more to teach us than the fact of warfare. It gives us a model for the battle. It is especially significant to note that Israel never won a conflict because they had more soldiers, more effective weapons, or better strategies than the enemy. It was the Lord who made the difference every time. It was God who drove out the enemy before Israel. In every battle it was *spiritual* power that determined who won. But God didn't act while Israel was sitting in camp, at least not very often. He always gave Israel something to do. They had to go out and make contact with the enemy, and their orders from God sometimes involved humanly foolish, high-risk things like marching around a double-walled city thirteen times, blowing their trumpets, and shouting and expecting something to happen (Joshua 6), or sending the choir out in front of the army against "a vast host" from Ammon, Moab, and Mount Seir (2 Chronicles 20). On other occasions their orders involved actual armed encounter. It appears that He never had them confront an enemy the same way twice. The obvious purpose of this was to keep them aware that it was not human strength or cleverness which was accomplishing victory—it was God!

Anyone who has been involved in direct encounters with the demonic world will recognize the similarities. It is always God who makes the difference, not us; and He seems to have an infinite number of ways of doing it. How-to-do-it manuals have only limited value in this war. An open relationship with our Lord which gives us an ability to discern His leading is imperative.

When Israel didn't bother to ask God what to do, they got into trouble. Their defeat at Ai and their deception by the Gibeonites are clear examples of that (Joshua 7, 9). (Joshua 9:14 says, "The men of Israel sampled their provisions but did not inquire of the Lord.") In fact, when His people failed to do it God's way, God even allowed the enemy to put them to shame in stinging defeat (cf. Judges 2:10-15). Likewise, today some who have thought their protection was automatic or who have taken the idea of spiritual warfare lightly have found themselves dealing with defeat they never thought possible.

Power Encounter

Spiritual warfare in this dimension is frequently referred to as power encounter in missiological literature. The phrase was probably first used by Alan Tippett. One of the earliest uses of the term was in his book *Verdict Theology*, published in 1969. One chapter in this book is entitled "Universalism or Power Encounter," and in it he says: "The Scriptures leave us with a clear picture of a battle being fought, of a conflict of powers, with a verdict of victory or defeat for mansoul [sic]."[1] In his book *People Movements in Southern Polynesia*, published in 1972, the term occurs several times. While he gives illustrations of power encounters, he does not give a general definition of the term.

Tippett makes it clear, however, that he sees a significant link between power encounter and the growth of the Church. In a summary statement he says:

> At the level of actual conversion from paganism . . . no matter how many elements may be woven into the conversion complex in communal society, the group action . . . must fix itself in encounter at some material locus of power at some specific point of time. . . . Where such demonstrations occur churches begin to grow.[2]

The big question in missions circles tends to be how prominent a place power encounters should have in missionary or evangelistic ministry, if indeed they have any place at all. Are they normative; that is, are they to be expected on a constant basis? Are they occasional occurrences? Or are we out of line even talking about such things? The balance philosophy enunciated earlier places me somewhere near the center of this spectrum of views. The powerlessness of such large segments of the contemporary evangelical Church does not seem to fit the Biblical requirement to demonstrate the glory of God. On the other hand, the expectation that church life is a constant round of supernatural manifestations does not seem to fit the picture of the Church found in the Scriptures.

Some illustrations of power encounters would more accurately be seen as encounters of truth with superstition. The animistic concepts of power are often not Biblical, and their explanation systems for the world in which they live are often full of wrong information and wrong assumptions.

Our Western worldviews tend to put most references to supernatural activity or spirit activity into the category of superstition. If the worldview set forth in this book is accurate, there is real spirit power with which we need to be prepared to deal. If we can demonstrate that Christianity gives us the power to overcome the evil spirits which operate in our world, this will provide an answer both to the superstitions and to the real spirits with which we are in confrontation.

Power encounter is sometimes presented as a necessary component in successful evangelism and church planting. Depending on one's definition of power encounter, that may or may not be true. If prayer is included in the concept of power encounter, I would agree that such an encounter is necessary, and I will present a case for that later. If, however, power encounter is seen only in overt encounters between power exercised by evil spirits and power exercised by God through His servants, then I do not think that power encounter is always necessary.

The idea is sometimes set forth that when people see God work miracles, they will be more apt to believe. There are Biblical examples of that happening (Acts 5:12-14; 8:4-8; 13:11, 12), but there are also examples of that not happening (John 6:36; 7:5; 15:24; Acts 14:8ff.; 16:16-24). Jesus often did not fare well in spite of His miracles, and Paul went through all kinds of suffering at the hands of people who saw the signs and wonders he did.

There will always be those who will reject the truth no matter what the form in which it is presented. Jesus told us to expect that (Matthew 7:13, 14; John 15:18-25). But He cast out demons and healed people anyway, and He commanded His followers to do the same. And He is healing through His people today—not at the same level of gifting He possessed, but He is healing. Further, He is giving people victory over the power of evil spirits today.

The point is, we live in a world where spiritual

power is still the real power behind what happens, and we need to be prepared to operate in the sphere of the power of God under His divine leadership. As we learn from the experience of Israel at Ai in the Old Testament, we must not make our own assessment of the situation and calculate the human resources needed to accomplish a given task and expect to be successful. We ought rather to seek His evaluation of the situation and look to Him for the resources to carry out His purposes. Unless we can demonstrate His power to meet the circumstances of life, we will not have a very appealing message to most of the world. As we have already said, that demonstration may be anything from coping with the pressures of daily life to casting out demons, but the power must be there.

CHAPTER ELEVEN

STANDING AGAINST SATAN'S SCHEMES

POWER ENCOUNTER HAS BEEN thought of primarily in terms of missionary ministry, but that is changing. Most of the areas we formerly talked about only in cross-cultural situations we now are confronting in our own cultural setting. It is probably true that those who work with the victims of the rising tide of occult activity in this country see it more than those who are not so involved, but there can be no doubt that open demonic activity is on the increase. In any case, Christians need to be aware of the dimensions of our warfare as a basis for prayer, if nothing else.

We will now consider the ways in which the Church should be involved in aggressively challenging the devil's claim as "the god of this age [or world]" (2 Corinthians 4:4) and in rescuing people from his grip.

Evangelism

The Church has many legitimate functions, but none is more basic than evangelism—bringing people "from the dominion of darkness . . . into the kingdom of the Son he loves" (Colossians 1:13). And this is always a power encounter. It involves moving from one sphere of power to another—from Satan's to God's. While spiritual power is always involved in conversion, in the animistic world this will be understood much more clearly than in most areas of the Western world.

As we have already noted, the seeking of power is often a key factor in the decision of an individual or group to leave a non-Christian religion and to embrace Christianity. While that may be less true in the West, it is even becoming that way here. Paul describes conversion viewed from one perspective as moving "from the power of Satan to God" (Acts 26:18). It is in this sense that evangelism involves a power encounter. We need, therefore, to include in our theology of conversion the concept of power—moving from one realm of power (Satan's) to another realm of power (God's) and a definition of where one is going to look for power to meet the crises of life. Our theology obviously needs to include a great deal more than that, and the basis of salvation must be broader than that. But since this is where so many people begin in their thinking about life, we need to be prepared to meet them where they are.

There is evidence that in the Early Church the preparation of converts for baptism included clear teaching on the subject of relations to Satan and demons, that candidates went through some form of exorcism (or deliverance), and that the baptismal service itself was a dramatization of this change of loyalties. We are told that after the opening ceremony the candidates would enter the baptistery, kneel down in humble acknowledgment of their slavery to sin and Satan, and turn their faces to the West (the region of the sun's departure and therefore of darkness and of demons). Then the candidates would make a bold declaration as though the devil himself were present: "I renounce thee, Satan, and all thy service and all thy works." Then they would blow at the devil as a symbol of driving him away. It is reported that St. Ambrose required the candidates to spit in the devil's face as a clear act of renunciation and their unquestioned position of authority in Christ.[1]

Then the persons being baptized would turn to the East, the symbol of the resurrected and victorious Christ, and affirm their new loyalty in such words as, "I enter into Your service, O Christ." This service also frequently included laying on of hands and anointing with oil to emphasize three key truths: deliverance from demonic power, cleansing by the blood of Christ, and filling with the Holy Spirit. We still talk about the last two of these truths, but the elimination of the renunciation of the devil by baptismal candidates is another reflection of the Western worldview with its lack of a functional view of demons. It is not difficult to see, however, how functional such a concept and such a baptismal ceremony would be to converts coming to Christ from the practice of animism and many of the folk religions.

The point needs to be made that this is not just a matter of contextualizing Christianity to the belief system of the people to whom one ministers. A break with any ungodly spiritual heritage and establishing one's spiritual inheritance based on adoption into God's family ought to be a part of the conversion process anywhere. It often becomes one of the early steps in the counseling process.

For example, a student couple came to me one day saying that they would like to be missionaries to Africa but that the wife's physical condition would probably prevent it. In talking with them, I discovered that she had some history of occult activity in her family, including the practice of a form of magical healing. I counseled them to renounce this and any other things out of their past which God might show them, and to affirm their position in Christ against any demonic powers at work. They did this, and immediately the wife's condition began to improve. They went to Africa on a short-term basis with a student team, and the wife flourished there. Today they are on permanent assignment in Africa.

The failure to deal with this critical issue at the time of conversion and baptism is closely connected to the syncretism which has developed on most mission fields. When we fail to take seriously the work of Satan and demons and do not apply the power of the Cross against them, they continue to carry on their harassment against people even if those people have become believers. Protection is not automatic, and the demons are glad to take advantage of any weaknesses or wrong beliefs on our part.

The Destruction of Occult Objects

Closely related to this renunciation of one's spiritual inheritance and one's personal involvement in occult activity is the cleansing of one's person and dwelling of any objects related to such a belief system. This is what was behind the burning of the scrolls related to sorcery in Acts 19. This is not only symbolic of one's break with such practices; it is an open challenge to the demonic powers behind them to defend themselves if they can. We have already discussed the relationship between physical objects and demons; namely, the object has no power in itself. We also took a brief look at superstition. To assume, however, that there is therefore never any power involved allows the demons to continue to mediate their power through the object.

Also related to this is the challenging of power thought to reside in totem animals, birds, or reptiles. Alan Tippett speaks of this type of power encounter in his writings on the subject. He tells, for example, about a chief in Polynesia who had become a believer, but who had been singularly unsuccessful in convincing other leaders he had made the right decision and that they should follow him in it. He finally decided to demonstrate the power of his new faith by challenging the spirits behind a sacred turtle by eating the flesh of that turtle. When he did this and nothing happened to him, the response of his people changed. Tippett reports:

> The demonstration [of Christ's power] became a reference point for subsequent action by people who desired to change their religion. What they had heard with no great conviction from itinerant preachers suddenly became dramatically relevant. A great door opened to the missionaries.[2]

Some would say that the "demonstration" showed there was never any power in the totem animal in the first place, that it was just superstition right from the start. We have been singularly unsuccessful in convincing persons coming from animistic belief systems of that fact, even after extensive education. An African student told me, for example, that in his country, which is one the more advanced nations in Africa both educationally and in terms of the percentage of professed Christians, a leading attorney died, and his widow was making arrangements for his burial when leaders from the man's tribe showed up to claim the body.

They insisted that it must be buried in tribal territory or they would have major problems with the spirits. The wife was not from that tribe, and she insisted that he be buried in the city where he worked and where he died. The case finally ended in the highest court of that country, and Christian leaders who were called as witnesses affirmed that it was important to bury the body in tribal territory to avoid problems with the spirit world.

This type of syncretism is present in major segments of the Church, and it is there because we have not dealt forthrightly with the issue of spiritual power. If spirit power is real, it takes real power to overcome it. Christ provides that power, and there is therefore no basis for fear of what spirits—real or imagined—can do to us. Good theology on this point takes care of the real thing and of superstition as well.

Healing

Another aspect of ministry which involves the demonstration of power is healing. This subject has been widely discussed, and I will not attempt even a summary of other positions, nor do I suppose that what I will say is going to settle the issue. I am convinced, however, that the missionary who is not prepared to trust God for healing of physical conditions will find it difficult to convince people with an animistic base to their belief system that Christianity is really a religion of power.

There can be no doubt that healing was an integral part of the ministry of Jesus, and I agree with James Kallas who argues in his book *The Significance of the Synoptic Miracles* that healing and dealing with demons were not aspects of ministry unique to Him in order to confirm His identity as Messiah and to validate His message, though they did both of those things. They were, nevertheless, an integral part of His ministry. Driving back the power of the usurper "god of this world" was accomplished by the demonstration of God's power as well as by the proclamation of His truth, and those two elements of ministry continue to be valid today, especially on the frontiers of mission where the Church is just being planted.

I am aware of the arguments that say such "miracles" were unique to certain periods in Biblical history and that they cannot be expected today. I find the arguments unconvincing, however, especially when talking about planting the Church in areas of the world where it has not been previously. It appears clear that God is using healing and the casting out of demons to attest to the truthfulness of the gospel message today just as He did in apostolic times and that such ministries are still a vital part of our total ministry, not just a confirmation of the verbal message. Our faith must be based in truth, not just in miracles; but part of the truth is that God does indeed still work in power in all areas of life.

The experience of the church in Mainland China is a dramatic example of this. For example, in 1983 the following report appeared:

> In a certain village in Henan province . . . there were only six Christians one year ago. Today that number has increased to over one thousand. . . .
>
> The villagers gave two reasons for this extraordinary phenomenon: 1) Many signs and miracles appeared there. A young village girl, declared dead at a hospital and showing no signs of life for three days, recovered, and a man crippled for 18 years was healed. 2) There were good leaders there who spoke out with boldness and authority.[3]

So significant were these demonstrations of power that the Communist officials in Henan Province drew up a set of guidelines for the Church which included, "Do not pray for the sick or exorcise demons."[4]

Similar accounts could be given from a number of other parts of the world. It seems very evident that God is prepared to do, and in fact is doing, far more than our worldview or our faith has viewed as possible. The completion of the task of planting the Church among all peoples requires that we be in touch with our Commander.

He is still giving victory over the enemy through His own divine power.

Having said this, however, we must recognize that human suffering is caused by many different things; and it is necessary to take the cause into account when seeking healing. Physical suffering may be caused by injury, by genetically transmitted disease, by organisms in our environment, by emotions, by sin, by demons, and by divine providence. Providence is involved to some extent in all cases. My point, however, is that God always wants to deal with basic causes, not just symptoms. For example, it will do no good to pray for healing which is caused by sin if we are not willing to deal with the sin.

A classic illustration of this is given by David Seamands. Seamands was a second-generation missionary in India. He also had problems with serious asthma attacks. He had been prayed for in the past with no change. Then one day he read that resentment could cause things like asthma. That was interesting, but he was sure that he had dealt with his sin long ago, and he was certain he was not holding on to any resentments. As he tried to press on with his reading the Lord kept saying, "What about your mother?" In desperation he finally asked his wife if she had noticed any strained relationship with his mother. She said she had, but that it was a little too delicate to talk about. So Seamands began working through his feelings about his mother. As he did, he became aware that he was no longer having asthma attacks.[5] Healing in this case was not a matter of a miracle in response to faith; it was an act of God in response to obedience. But without the obedience, in the form of forgiveness, God could not have answered the prayer for healing.

The experience of Paul in Lystra provides a good Biblical model for how healing fits into ministry. The Scriptures tell us that one of the men listening to Paul preach was a congenital cripple and that when Paul met his gaze, he "saw that he had faith to be healed" (Acts 14:8-10). Paul did not then say, "I have the gift of healing, so I will go heal a few people"—he apparently did not go around Lystra healing everyone. He simply responded to the Holy Spirit's prompting. The Holy Spirit was giving him the gift of healing as He—the Holy Spirit—willed (1 Corinthians 12:11).

A contemporary illustration of this comes from the Indonesian revival of a few years ago. After reporting on the instances of healing which he investigated there, Kurt Koch says, "This does not mean that members of the teams can heal people whenever they want to, but rather that they ask the Lord concerning each individual case."[6] Much harm has been done to people when well-intentioned friends have tried to claim healing for them or to cast demons out of them before they have talked with God about the case and gotten to the basis of the problem. We sometimes forget the lesson of the battle of Ai: you can't expect God to act in power when sin has not been dealt with.

It is indeed true that the Christian life is the exciting process of trying to keep your balance, and it is never more true than in this area of ministry.

Open Confrontation

Another type of power encounter which may become part of a missionary ministry is open confrontation with practitioners of occult arts. Paul faced this in Paphos with Elymas the sorcerer. The power encounter which ensued demonstrated that the power of God was far greater than any power known to Elymas, and it had a significant role in the proconsul coming to faith. Luke tells us, "When the proconsul saw what had happened, he believed, for he was amazed at the teaching about the Lord" (Acts 13:12).

I first learned of this through missionary literature many years ago, specifically the biography of John Paton. Paton was a pioneer missionary in the New Hebrides Islands. This was before the days of airplanes or radio. When the sailing ship dropped you off on one of those islands, you were there at least until another sailing ship paid a call to the island. There were not many options available in an emergency. In such a setting, Paton was speaking in a village one evening to a small group of people. He recognized in the circle three men who were known to be the most powerful sorcerers in the area. They had demonstrated their power many times.

When Paton finished his message, these men said to him, "Missionary, we don't need your Jehovah. We can kill you by the power of Nahak"—"Nahak" being the name of one of the spirits from whom they got their power. What does a missionary do at such a time? Paton's options were indeed few. He also did not have the luxury of a well-lighted room filled with fellow Christians as the setting for his decision. The missionary, however, did not hesitate. He knew that these people believed in and practiced contagious magic. (That is the belief that something which has been in touch with a person's body continues to be in touch with it and can therefore be treated as an extension of one's body.) So Paton took three pieces of fruit, took a bite out of each, and gave the rest of the fruit to the three sorcerers with this public challenge:

> "You have seen me eat of this fruit; you have seen me give the remainder to your Sacred Men; they have said they can kill me by Nahak, but I challenge them to do it if they can, without arrow or spear, club or musket; for I deny that they have any power against me . . . by their sorcery."[7]

When after a week these three demonized men were unable to do any harm to Paton—when they tried to resort to spears, God froze their arms in the air so they could not throw them—you may be sure that the people "heard" the gospel with a clarity with which they did not hear it simply coming from the mouth of the missionary.

Abou had been a Muslim sorcerer in Burkina Faso before his conversion, but after receiving basic teaching from the Mennonite missionaries who had led him to Christ, he began ministering to his people. It was not long, however, until the sorcerers in the area began to try to get rid of Abou. The change in his life and the credibility of his witness was having a profound impact on his people. After a number of dramatic but unsuccessful attempts on his life, a woman named Makoura, reputed to be the most powerful sorceress in the whole area, invited Abou to come to her village to preach. Her power was reported to be from an evil spirit who had enabled her to kill hundreds of people. Her real purpose in the invitations was obviously something other than to hear Abou preach. Loren Entz reports what happened this way:

This trip was made on a borrowed bicycle. Abou carried a tape player, cassette tapes, Bible pictures, and a change of clothes. Suddenly, with an explosive noise, the bicycle burst into flames. Abou miraculously escaped unharmed with the Christian teaching materials, but everything else burned. Even sand wouldn't put out the fire immediately. So Abou continued on foot to his destination.

On arrival, Makoura exclaimed, "What are you doing here? You are supposed to be dead."

Abou answered, "You invited me, and I've come with the power of Jesus." Abou was invited to share this source of power with Makoura. He spent the night in the house of the evil spirit which was no

longer able to live there. It had not been victorious
in the power encounter with Abou's Jesus.[8]

Many people have no worldview categories into
which to plug such a story with any meaning. The fact
is, however, that Makoura later became a Christian, as
did many others in that area—something which I don't
think would have happened had not someone been prepared to confront the enemy personally with a demonstration of Christ's power.

The Bible does not commission us to go on a "lion"
hunt in order to create such situations, but it is very clear
that we are to be prepared with the faith and the courage
required to meet such confrontations victoriously when
we do meet them.

Casting Out Demons

One of the more obvious types of power encounter is the
casting out of demons. Unfortunately, not many missionaries or evangelists or pastors enter their ministries
prepared to handle demonic problems. On the mission
field, it is often assumed that national pastors will be able
to take care of such situations, but that is not always true,
especially if they have been educated in Western mis-
sionary-run schools. It is true, however, that the demonstration of power in such confrontations may be a key to
unlocking an apparently resistant people group.

For example, there had been a Christian witness
among the Chinese in West Kalimantan (formerly
Borneo) for many years. Immigrants from China had
brought their faith with them, and there were a couple
of struggling congregations of believers. The Communist
takeover of China had brought divisions in the Chinese
community which spilled over into the Church. The
Overseas Missionary Fellowship (formerly China Inland

Mission) superintendent in Indonesia at the time says of the situation:

> Being traders and financiers, few had any time for spiritual things and showed little interest in the Gospel. On the other hand, old and young, rich and poor, they lived all their lives subject to bondage, slaves to Satan and his emissaries, and in constant fear of evil spirits which were as real to them as the wealth they possessed.[9]

When OMF decided to enter this field in 1952, they were told that "it was impossible to expect any spiritual results working under such conditions," and for the first years of their ministry there that seemed like the truth. They had seen a total of five converts during that time. George Steed, the field superintendent, says:

> However, something began to happen; and, in the next few short years, more than 1,500 men and women came into a personal saving experience of the grace of God. Political barriers were broken down; hearts hardened by years of rejecting the Gospel were melted; lives which had been wholly given over to serving the devil were made new and surrendered to the Lord for willing service. Young people joined together to form evangelistic bands and responded to urgent invitations to come and bring the Gospel to country villages. Other young people dedicated their lives for full-time service and sought training in Bible schools and colleges. Some have gone to other islands as home missionaries.[10]

West Kalimantan became one of the bright spots in OMF work, and the Church flourished. When asked what accounted for this, Steed replied:

We do not overlook the years of preparation and patient, faithful seed-sowing, or the watering of the seed by the faithful prayers of saints around the world; but *we believe it is not just coincidental that when the Lord's servants commenced openly to challenge the power of darkness and, in the name of our victorious Lord, command the demons to come out of the possessed ones, the gates of hell began to yield and captives were set free.*[11]

I do not propose this as the cure-all for difficult fields, but it remains to be seen how many other "resistant peoples" may be opened to the gospel through a willingness to take seriously demonic control over people.

The warfare in which we Christians are all engaged does indeed demand that we take an offensive posture in relation to the enemy. We are commissioned to invade his territory, not just wait for him to attack us.

CHAPTER TWELVE

THE ULTIMATE WEAPON

"PRAYER IS WHERE THE action is. Any church without a well organized and systematic prayer program is simply operating a religious treadmill."[1] Those are strong words, but they take us right to the heart of the spiritual warfare in which we are engaged. The Church's prayer program needs not only to be well-organized and systematic, it needs to be based on a correct theology and worldview. Too often pastors talk only about how many people are in prayer meeting, not about whether people are really learning to pray and whether prayers are being answered. The bottom line of prayer may be whether we pray to a God who is in sovereign control over the universe and whether we believe that He is able to give us victory over the forces of darkness with which we wrestle.

I used to picture prayer as spiritual support activity, something like the quartermaster corps in the army that sends supplies to the troops on the front lines in time of war. In one of our combat assignments during the Second World War, the troops who were supposed to be supplying us with the materials for our front-line activity did not have the same sense of urgency as those on the front lines; as a result we had rationing in our unit to the extent that the artillery units were primarily using captured enemy guns and ammunition. (The chaplain for whom I served as an assistant was not even given a gasoline ration because he was not considered strategic to the operation of the unit.) People who don't pray for those on the front lines of spiritual ministry are sometimes likened to the supply troops who failed to get the supplies to us. I now see that picture a bit differently.

Prayer is not a rear-echelon activity; prayer is front-lines spiritual warfare. It is the ultimate weapon in our "struggle . . . against the rulers, against the authorities, against the powers of this dark world and against the spiritual forces of evil in the heavenly realms" (Ephesians 6:12). It is as S. D. Gordon says in *Quiet Talks on Prayer*: "Prayer is striking the winning blow at the concealed enemy. Service is gathering up the results of that blow among the [people] we see and touch."[2] In a sense it would be correct to say that prayer is not simply a weapon we use; it is the battle. That is why persevering prayer is so difficult for most of us.

Earlier we said there is a way for every Christian to be involved in pressing the battle against the enemy on the very front lines. It is not just missionaries and full-time workers who do this. It is rather every Christian who prays!

One other key concept, however, needs to be considered before we look more specifically at prayer as the ultimate weapon in the battle in which we are all engaged.

Dealing with Territorial Demons

An area of spiritual warfare which is just beginning to be taken seriously is the confrontation of demons associated with specific locations or geopolitical units. The whole concept of the gods of the nations in the Old Testament, including the references in Daniel to the prince of Persia and the prince of Greece (Daniel 10:13, 20), provide us with a Biblical perspective on this. Jesus' statement about binding "the strong man" (Matthew 12:29) and the New Testament references to the principalities and powers may also apply.

I have come to believe that Satan does indeed assign a demon or a corps of demons to every geopolitical unit in the world and that they are among the principalities and powers against whom we wrestle. For me, this concept first came up in a missionary context when I read of a new missionary going into an American Indian village in Canada. A veteran of such ministry told him that he had better be prepared to do battle with the demon of the village on his arrival. The young missionary's worldview and training had not prepared him for such concepts, and the new missionary and his family moved in without further thought. It was not long, however, before his wife became ill and had to be flown out. Later his son became ill and had to be flown out as well. The young man was standing alone in his cabin with his back to the stove to keep warm when he heard an awful noise that seemed to be coming from the stovepipe. Suddenly something jumped on his back. Although he couldn't see anything, he was barely able to stagger to a chair to sit down. The "thing" identified itself as the demon of the village, and the battle was joined. The missionary knew enough to claim his position in Christ, and he said, "All right, you guardian angel of this village, let's have it out. Jesus Christ sent me here. I might die, but I am not leaving. In the Lord's hands are the issues of life and death." After thirty minutes of struggle, claiming the legal victory of Calvary and all the while gasping for breath, the demon left as it had come, and the missionary stayed on to carry out his ministry.[3]

Those associated with Bible translation have told me that their translation teams seem to experience special difficulties at two points in their work. The first is when they first enter a new tribe, and the other is when the completed New Testament is delivered. It is obvious why Satan would provoke special difficulties at these two times. He is not about to sit idly by and see his territory invaded by the army of the Lord against whom he has rebelled and to see God's truth become available to offset the lies through which he has maintained control over the people in that tribe or nation.

How this may relate to many other missionary problems we simply do not know because it has not even been seen as being in the realm of possibility. More recently, however, some other things have called this to our attention. For example, there is a town on the boundary between Brazil and Uruguay in which the main street is the international border. One side of the street is in Brazil and the other in Uruguay. Ralph Mahoney of World MAP tells of a missionary who was in this town passing out tracts. On the Uruguay side of the street people were very unresponsive. They would routinely refuse the tracts or almost immediately throw them away. But then he noticed that a person who had refused a tract on the Uruguay side of the street crossed over to the Brazil side and accepted the tract and even thanked the missionary profusely for it. This aroused his curiosity; so he did some structured observation and discovered that the same pattern was followed by several more people. Peter Wagner reports that

> later as [the missionary] was praying about the incident, the words of Jesus came to his mind: "No one can enter a strong man's house and plunder his goods, unless he first binds the strong man, and then he will plunder the house" (Mark 3:27). Could it be that the "strong man" on the Brazilian side had been

bound while the "strong man" on the Uruguayan side was still exercising power?[4]

The idea of a particular spirit being associated with a particular geographical location or a particular cultural group is a familiar concept among tribal peoples generally.

Our two-level worldview results in a tendency to separate the spiritual and natural worlds and makes the idea that a spirit would have enough involvement with the affairs of a particular place to be considered the controlling spirit seem strange. There are Biblical indications, however, that God's plan included the assignment of an angel to each nation.[5] Satan being a counterfeiter, he has simply copied this pattern by assigning one of the fallen angels to parallel God's pattern of government.

This concept does not seem to be prominent in the New Testament, but depending again on one's worldview, the "principalities and powers" of the New Testament may well be seen as fitting into this pattern. Our cultural "glasses" may make this difficult to bring into focus.

In any case, territorial spirits are not to be a primary focus of our lives or ministries because they are not presented that way in the Scriptures. But an understanding that this is indeed part of the structure of the enemy's kingdom gives perspective to our battle strategy and, I believe, especially to our praying.

Prayer as Warfare

The amazing revival movement that has been in process in Argentina illustrates this point. Edgardo Silvoso, writing in *Global Church Growth*, reports that 3,000, and maybe as many as 8,000, persons per day were making decisions for Christ in Argentina at the time he was writing. One of the key elements in the evangelistic approach which seems to be new is the role of prayer. Not only are prayer brigades organized to support the evangelists and not only is prayer a prominent part of the services, but at least one of the evangelists will spend from several days up to two weeks in fasting and prayer to bind "the strong man or the 'prince' who controls the darkness of that particular 'cosmos'" prior to beginning the crusade.[6] As soon as the Lord gives him the assurance that this has been done, he begins preaching. The results speak for themselves. This is a dramatic illustration of S. D. Gordon's statement, "Intercession is winning the victory over the chief, and service is taking the field after the chief is driven off."[7]

There are other elements to the evangelistic ministries in Argentina which help to account for the response. One of them is the seriousness with which the workers take the whole concept of spiritual warfare. This is reflected in the way they pray, but it is also seen, among other ways , in the use of an "intensive care" tent where the demonized are ministered to. Many evangelicals have chosen simply to ignore the demonic manifestations or to avoid confrontation with or ministry to spiritists. But where that challenge is being met head-on, God's power is clearly demonstrated, and many are drawn to Him.

Silvoso reports that when Carlos Anacondia, one of the leading evangelists in Argentina, went to the city of Cordoba, they told him that this was a sophisticated, educational center and that his style of evangelism would not be received. The prayer meetings were held, and the crusade began. After two months, more than 50,000 decisions for Christ had been recorded in Cordoba.[8]

The real issue at stake in what is called "warfare praying" is still the glory of God. My observation of the prayers that I hear in most of the churches I attend or in which I minister (and, all too often, even of my own prayers) is that they are relatively "small" prayers. We ask for daily needs and "mercy drops," but we seldom ask for whole nations. Not many pray like John Knox: "Give me Scotland or I die!" Is this not because we have lost the concept of Yahweh as Lord of the nations? Are our prayers not a reflection of our concept of the one to whom we pray? A familiar bit of verse says:

> Thou art coming to a King;
> Large petitions with thee bring.
> For His grace and power are such
> None can ever ask too much.

If most of our prayers are really a reflection of our concept of the glory and power of our God, our theology is in serious need of overhaul.

In the final analysis, the question is not whether there are demons assigned to the "nations," but whether our God is big enough to handle any and all of them. Many of the great prayer warriors in the history of the Church have not reflected a conscious concept of territorial spirits, but they have moved the heart of God to overcome the power of such spirits—spirits that bind the minds of unbelievers—and to free those held captive by them.

It is also probable that Paul Billheimer is correct when he says that the most powerful kind of praying is praise. Praise, he contends, is the best way to develop faith because it focuses on the character of God, and it is faith which ultimately overcomes the enemy.[9] So warfare praying is not ultimately a negative kind of praying— that is, praying *against* territorial spirits. It is a supremely positive kind of praying in the form of affirmations of the sovereign power of God, the unending nature of His love, and the victory of Calvary over all God's enemies.

However, Jesus taught that we cannot plunder a "strong man's house" unless we first bind the strong man (Matthew 12:29). That concept seems to be in the context of ministry to individuals, but the principle is the same in ministry to people groups. Some would like to reduce this matter of binding to a single authoritative command uttered by the Christian. I think binding, especially in dealing with territorial demons, is a process. That process is prevailing, intercessory prayer—the kind of prayer described by Wesley Duewel in his book *Mighty, Prevailing Prayer*[10] and by Thomas White in the paper he gave at Lausanne II.

Sometimes binding is presented in such a way that it appears we can go around binding the spirits controlling any area we choose. I do not think that is the case. I do think, however, that when God commissions a church or a missionary team to minister in a particular location, that church or those missionaries and the prayer team ministering with them can claim the authority of our Lord through intercessory prayer over every spirit of the enemy claiming that territory for Satan. God is still the God of the nations, and He is still in the business of answering the prayers of His people at top levels of spiritual power.

Our worldview often gets in the way here as in other areas of spiritual warfare. We are simply not convinced that spirits get things done in the world for good or for ill.

Sometimes we hear people say, "I can't preach; I can't teach; I can't sing; about all I can do is pray." That is like a soldier saying, "I don't have a machine gun or a bazooka or a cannon; all I have is an intercontinental ballistic missile."

Gordon has it right when he says, "Prayer is striking

the winning blow at the concealed enemy. Service is gathering up the results of that blow among the [people] we see and touch." Many Christians have become very discouraged because they have difficulty maintaining a vital prayer life. They blame themselves and their lack of discipline for their problems—and these factors do indeed contribute to the problem. Our failure to recognize the warfare aspects of prayer, however, is more often the cause of our problems and is testimony to the success of Satan's strategy to keep the Church from understanding just how critical prayer is in this warfare and thus to produce both ineffective praying and discouragement. This is especially true as it relates to genuine intercession.

The founder of the seminary I attended used to say, "Prayer works; prayer is work; and prayer leads to work." Prayer is even more than work. It is *war*. One does not go onto the front lines in war and not expect to get shot at. I was on the front lines in the Second World War. I was on the receiving end of enemy fire. I saw my friends wounded and killed. War is not fun and games. You can't turn it off like you can a television. So when we begin to take intercession for the unreached peoples of the world (and of our own nation and neighborhood) seriously, we can expect to find ourselves on the front lines of the battle—face to face with the enemy.

In Luke 18 Jesus told His disciples a parable "to show them that they should always pray and not give up" (v. 1). The parable is about a widow who took her case against an adversary to the judge. The language indicates that she knew she was on the right side of the law, and she was demanding justice. Although the judge tried to ignore her, her persistence finally paid off, and she got justice. The parable ends with the somewhat strange question, "However, when the Son of Man comes, will he find faith on the earth?" (v. 8b).

Faith doesn't seem to have been the issue in the

parable. It was the dogged persistence of the widow. The character often overlooked in the parable is the adversary; the faith commended is the kind of faith which holds out against the adversary. Based on this model, prayer becomes finding the will of God and insisting on it against the enemy.

The Old Testament parallel is Daniel's prayer in chapter 10. When the angel came with the answer to Daniel's prayer he said, "Do not be afraid, Daniel. Since the first day that you set your mind to gain understanding and to humble yourself before your God, your words were heard, and I have come in response to them. But the prince of the Persian kingdom withstood me twenty-one days. Then Michael, one of the chief princes, came to help me . . ." (vv. 12, 13). In the parable Jesus said that God would avenge His own "quickly," and in Daniel we are told that God started the answer on its way the first time Daniel prayed. Daniel's answer was delayed, however, because of warfare in the spiritual realm; so he had to fast and pray for twenty-one days. Jesus is asking if we have the kind of faith that is willing to persevere in prayer as Daniel did. That is the kind of praying which binds the strong man and sees the will of God done.

In this model, prayer is not just Jesus and me having a friendly visit. If it starts that way, it soon involves an enemy who is determined to keep that visit from getting to the point of releasing God's power against him and of reclaiming territory from him for the cause of Christ. Satan is not unduly threatened by the kind of prayer that stays within the Christian community. As long as we are not expelling him from the lives of people, he will let us be as religious as we wish. But if we begin to take seriously our call to Christian service and especially our commission to world evangelization—I speak advisedly—all hell may break loose.

This is why people say to me, "When I was a carnal

Christian and not really working at my Christian life, I didn't have these problems. Now that I have committed my life to Christ and am becoming more involved in ministry, I seem to have no end of problems. How come?" My response is, "Welcome to the war."

Yes, prayer is indeed striking the winning blow against the enemy, and we can expect to have a counterattack launched against us. But that should serve to convince us that prayer is a top priority in spiritual warfare. We need to make sure that when the Son of Man comes He will find faith on the earth.

Conclusion

The fact is, we are engaged in spiritual warfare whether we want to be or not. We may be winning or losing, but there is no way to declare neutrality. I have told the Lord many times that I would be glad for an honorable discharge; but that comes only when we are ready to go Home, and that time hasn't arrived for me. While I was in the army during the war, I saw many men who were more concerned with how they could get out of work than how they could bring the war to an end. I have already mentioned the time we were sitting on the front lines with almost no supplies, including ammunition, because the troops handling supplies did not have the same perspective on the war as those at the front. Too often that is a picture of the Church.

May the Church of Christ recognize the reality of the war in which we are engaged, the incomparable power which is available to us through the Cross, and the unavoidable responsibility to appropriate the power to carry out the commission of our Lord until His return signals the end of the war.

NOTES

CHAPTER ONE: *The Glory of God*

1. *Attack from the Spirit World* (Wheaton, IL: Tyndale House, 1973), pp. 203, 204.
2. Alan R. Tippett, "Probing Missionary Inadequacies at the Popular Level," in *International Review of Missions* 49 (October 1960), pp. 411-419.
3. C. Peter Wagner and F. Douglas Pennoyer, *Wrestling with Dark Angels* (Ventura, CA: Regal, 1990), p. 129.
4. Geoffrey Grogan, "Isaiah" in *The Expositor's Bible Commentary*, Volume 6, ed. Frank Gaebelein (Grand Rapids, MI: Zondervan/Regency Reference Library, 1986), p. 105.
5. Lewis Sperry Chafer, *Satan: His Motive and Methods* (Grand Rapids, MI: Zondervan, 1919), p. 74.
6. Grogan, "Isaiah," p. 106.
7. C. S. Lewis, *The Screwtape Letters* (New York: Macmillan, 1961), pp. 32, 33.
8. Marguerite Shuster, *Power, Pathology, Paradox* (Grand Rapids, MI: Zondervan/Academie Books, 1987), p. 156.

CHAPTER TWO: *Worldviews in Conflict*

1. James Sire, *The Universe Next Door* (Downers Grove, IL: InterVarsity Press, 1976), p. 17.
2. John W. Montgomery, ed., *Demon Possession* (Minneapolis: Bethany House, 1976), p. 215.
3. See Alan R., Tippett, "Evangelization Among Animists," in *Let the Earth Hear His Voice* (Minneapolis: Worldwide Publications, 1975), pp. 167, 168.
4. Paul Hiebert, "The Flaw of the Excluded Middle," in *Missiology* 10 (January 1982), pp. 35-47.

5. *Ibid.*
6. Lesslie Newbigin, *Honest Religion for Secular Man* (London: SCM Press, 1986).

CHAPTER THREE: *The Power and the Glory*

1. G. Ernest Wright, *The God Who Acts* (Chicago: H. Regnery, 1952).
2. James Kallas, *The Significance of the Synoptic Gospels* (Greenwich, CT: Seabury Press, 1961).
3. Neil Anderson, *The Bondage Breaker* (Eugene, OR: Harvest House, 1990), pp. 29, 30

CHAPTER FOUR: *Spiritual Power Good and Bad*

1. Whittaker Chambers, "The Devil," in *Life,* February 2, 1948, pp. 84, 85.
2. C. S. Lewis, *The Screwtape Letters* (New York: Macmillan, 1961), p. 9.
3. Author unknown.

CHAPTER FIVE: *The Power of the Cross*

1. Donald Jacobs, *Demons* (Scottsdale, PA: Herald Press, 1972), p. 34.
2. John W. Montgomery, ed., *Demon Possession* (Minneapolis: Bethany House, 1976), p. 335.
3. *Ibid.*

CHAPTER SIX: *Spiritual Authority*

1. *Demon Experiences in Many Lands* (Chicago: Moody Press, 1960), pp. 37-40.
2. John MacMillan, *The Authority of the Believer* (Harrisburg, PA: Christian Publications, 1980).

CHAPTER SEVEN: *The Christian Defensive*

1. Wilbur N. Pickering, "Spiritual Warfare." Unpublished paper, 1987, p. 3.
2. John Eccles, *The Neurophysiolgical Basis of the Mind* (Oxford, 1953).
3. *Ibid.,* p. 285.
4. Rosalind Goforth, *Goforth of China* (Grand Rapids, MI: Zondervan, 1937), pp. 87, 88.

CHAPTER EIGHT: *Attacks in the Physical Realm*

1. *Victory over the Powers of Darkness.* (Goldenrod, FL: World-wide Keswick, n.d.).

2. W. L. McLeod, *Fellowship with the Fallen* (Prince Albert, SK: Northern Canada Mission Press, n.d.), p. 84.

CHAPTER NINE: *Attacks in the Spiritual Realm*

1. John W. Montgomery, ed., *Demon Possession* (Minneapolis: Bethany House, 1976), p. 337.
2. Clifton and Alma McElheran, *Let the Oppressed Go Free* (Calgary, AB: published by the author, 1984), pp. 17, 18.
3. Leroy Smith, "Effectively Resisting Satan," an audiotape in the series *Workshop on Protection* (Houston, TX: Calvary Baptist Church [6511 Uvalde, 77049]).
4. C. Fred Dickason, *Demon Possession and the Christian* (Westchester, IL: Crossway, 1989), p. 162.

CHAPTER TEN: *The Christian Offensive*

1. Alan R. Tippett, *Verdict Theology in Missionary Theory* (Lincoln, IL: Lincoln Christian College Press, 1969), p. 88.
2. Alan R. Tippett, *People Movements in Southern Polynesia* (Chicago: Moody Press, 1971), p. 169.

CHAPTER ELEVEN: *Standing Against Satan's Schemes*

1. F. Van der Meer, *Augustine the Bishop* (New York: Harper and Row, 1965), p. 364; E. C. Whitaker, *The Baptismal Liturgy* (London: SPCK, 1981), pp. 17, 36, 37.
2. Alan R. Tippett, *People Movements in Southern Polynesia* (Chicago: Moody Press, 1971), p. 19.
3. *Chinese Around the World*, August 1983, p. 16.
4. C. Peter Wagner, *On the Crest of the Wave* (Ventura, CA: Regal Books, 1983), p. 136.
5. David Seamands, *Healing of Memories* (Wheaton, IL: Victor Books, 1985), pp. 152-154.
6. Kurt Koch, *Revival in Indonesia* (Grand Rapids, MI: Kregel, 1972), p. 150.
7. James Paton, *The Story of John G. Paton* (New York: American Tract Society, 1909), p. 125, 126.
8. Loren Entz, "Challenge to Abou's Jesus," in *Evangelical Missions Quarterly* 22 (January 1986), p. 49.
9. Robert Peterson, *Are Demons for Real?* (Chicago: Moody Press, 1972), p. 8.
10. *Ibid.*
11. *Ibid.*, pp. 8, 9.

CHAPTER TWELVE: *The Ultimate Weapon*

1. Paul Billheimer, *Destined for the Throne* (Fort Washington, PA: Christian Literature Crusade, 1975), p. 18.
2. S. D. Gordon, *Quiet Talks on Prayer* (Grand Rapids, MI: Baker, 1980), p. 19. The title of this book is not reflective of the powerful truth it contains.
3. *Attack from the Spirit World* (Chicago: Moody Press, 1973), pp. 127, 128.
4. C. Peter Wagner, "The Key to Victory Is Binding the 'Strong Man,'" in *Ministries Today*, November-December 1986, p. 84.
5. See C. Peter Wagner, "Territorial Spirits and World Missions," in *Evangelical Missions Quarterly* 25 (July 1989), pp. 278, 288, and Thomas White, "A Model for Discovering, Penetrating and Overcoming Ruling Principalities and Powers," a paper presented at the Lausanne II Congress on World Evangelization, Manila, July 11-20, 1990.
6. Edgardo Silvoso, "Prayer Power: The Turnaround in Argentina," in *Global Church Growth*, 24 (July-September 1987), p. 5.
7. Gordon, *Quiet Talks on Prayer*, p. 17.
8. Edgardo Silvoso, "Spiritual Warfare in Argentina and the 'Plan Resistencia,'" a paper presented at the Lausanne II Congress on World Evangelization, Manila, July 11-20, 1990.
9. Billheimer, *Destined for the Throne*, p. 126.
10. Wesley Duewel, *Mighty, Prevailing Prayer* (Grand Rapids, MI: Zondervan/Francis Asbury, 1990); John Dawson, *Taking Our Cities for God* (Lake Mary, FL: Creation House, 1990).

BIBLIOGRAPHY

Anderson, Neil. *Victory over the Darkness*. Ventura, CA: Regal, 1990.

____*The Bondage Breaker*. Eugene, OR: Harvest House, 1990.

Attack from the Spirit World. Wheaton, IL: Tyndale House, 1973.

Billheimer, Paul. *Destined for the Throne*. Ft. Washington, PA: Christian Literature Crusade, 1975.

Bubeck, Mark I. *The Adversary*. Chicago: Moody Press, 1974.

____*Overcoming the Adversary*. Chicago: Moody Press, 1984.

Chafer, Lewis Sperry. *Satan: His Motive and Methods*. Grand Rapids, MI: Zondervan, 1919.

Chambers, Whittaker. "The Devil," in *Life*, February 2, 1948, pp. 84, 85.

Chinese Around the World, August 1983, p. 16.

Dawson, John. *Taking Our Cities for God: How to Break Spiritual Strongholds*. Lake Mary, FL: Creation House, 1989.

Demon Experiences in Many Lands. Chicago: Moody Press, 1960.

Dickason, C. Fred. *Angels: Elect and Evil*. Chicago: Moody Press, 1975.

_____*Demon Possession and the Christian.* Westchester, IL: Crossway Books, 1989. (Original edition Chicago: Moody Press, 1987.)

Duewel, Wesley L. *Mighty, Prevailing Prayer.* Grand Rapids, MI: Zondervan/Francis Asbury, 1990.

Entz, Loren. "Challenges to Abou's Jesus," in *Evangelical Missions Quarterly* 22 (January 1986), pp. 46-50.

Goforth, Rosalind. *Goforth of China.* Grand Rapids, MI: Zondervan, 1937.

Gordon, S. D. *Quiet Talks on Prayer.* Grand Rapids, MI: Baker, 1980. (Original edition Old Tappan, NJ: Revell, 1904.)

Graham, Billy. *Angels: God's Secret Agents.* Garden City, NY: Doubleday, 1975.

Grogan, Geoffrey. "Isaiah," in *The Expositor's Bible Commentary*,Volume 6, Frank Gaebelein, ed. Grand Rapids, MI: Zondervan/Regency Reference Library, 1986.

Henry, Rodney. *The Filipino Spirit World.* Manila: OMF Publications, 1986.

Hiebert, Paul. "The Flaw of the Excluded Middle," in *Missiology* 10 (January 1982), pp. 35-47.

Jacobs, Donald. *Demons.* Scottsdale, PA: Herald Press, 1972.

Kallas, James. *The Significance of the Synoptic Miracles.* Greenwich, CT: Seabury Press, 1961.

Koch, Kurt. *Revival in Indonesia.* Grand Rapids, MI: Kregel, 1972.

Kraft, Charles. *Christianity with Power: Your Worldview and Your Experience of the Supernatural.* Ann Arbor, MI: Servant, 1989.

Lewis, C. S. *The Screwtape Letters.* New York: Macmillan, 1961.

McElheran, Clifton and Alma. *Let the Oppressed Go Free.* Published by the authors (3805 Marlborough Drive N.E., G204, Calgary, AB T2A 5M7, Canada), 1984.

McLeod, W. L. *Fellowship with the Fallen.* Prince Albert, SK: Northern Canada Mission Press, 1984.

MacMillan, John. *The Authority of the Believer.* Harrisburg, PA: Christian Publications, 1980.

Montgomery, John W., ed. *Demon Possession.* Minneapolis: Bethany House, 1976.

Newbigin, Lesslie. *Honest Religion for Secular Man.* London: SCM Press, 1986.

Newport, John P. "Satan and Demons: A Theological Perspective," in J. W. Montgomery, ed., *Demon Possession.* Minneapolis: Bethany House, 1976.

Paton, James. *The Story of John G. Paton.* New York: American Tract Society, 1909.

Penn-Lewis, Jessie. *War on the Saints* (unabridged edition). New York: Thomas E. Lowe, 1905.

Peterson, Robert. *Are Demons for Real?* Chicago: Moody Press, 1972. (Originally published as *Roaring Lion.* London: OMF Books, 1968.)

Peretti, Frank E. *This Present Darkness.* Westchester, IL: Crossway Books, 1986.

____*Piercing the Darkness.* Westchester, IL: Crossway Books, 1989.

Pickering, Wilbur N. "Spiritual Warfare." Unpublished manuscript, 1987.

Seamands, David. *Healing of Memories.* Wheaton, IL: Victor Books, 1985.

Shuster, Marguerite. *Power, Pathology, Paradox.* Grand Rapids, MI: Zondervan/Academie Books, 1987.

Silvoso, Edgardo. "Prayer Power: The Turnaround in Argentina," in *Church Global Growth* 24 (July-September 1987), pp. 4, 5.

____"Spiritual Warfare in Argentina and the 'Plan Resistencia.'" A paper presented at a Spiritual Warfare track workshop at Lausanne II Congress on World Evangelization held in Manila, Philippines, July 11-20, 1989.

Tippett, Alan R. "Probing Missionary Inadequacies at the Popular Level," in *International Review of Missions* 49 (October 1960), pp. 411-419.

____*Verdict Theology in Missionary Theory.* Lincoln, IL: Lincoln Christian College Press, 1969.

____*People Movements in Southern Polynesia.* Chicago: Moody Press, 1971.

____"Evangelization Among Animists," in *Let the Earth Hear His Voice.* Minneapolis: Worldwide Publications, 1975.

Van der Meer, F. *Augustine the Bishop.* New York: Harper and Row, 1965.

Victory over the Powers of Darkness. Goldenrod, FL: Worldwide Keswick, n.d.

Wagner, C. Peter. *On the Crest of the Wave.* Ventura, CA: Regal, 1983.

____"The Key to Victory Is Binding the 'Strong Man,'" in *Ministries Today,* November-December 1986, p. 84.

____"Territorial Spirits and World Missions," in *Evangelical Missions Quarterly* 25 (July 1989), pp. 278-288.

____ and Pennoyer, F. Douglas, editors. *Wrestling with the Dark Angels.* Ventura, CA: Regal, 1990.

Whitaker, E. C. *The Baptismal Liturgy.* London: SPCK, 1981.

White, Thomas B. "A Model for Discerning, Penetrating and Overcoming Ruling Principalities and Powers." Corvallis, OR: Frontline Ministries, 1989. A paper presented to the Spiritual Warfare track workshop at Lausanne II Congress on World Evangelization held in Manila, Philippines, July 11-20, 1989.

____*The Believer's Guide to Spiritual Warfare.* Ann Arbor, MI: Vine/Servant Publications, 1990.

Wimber, John. *Power Evangelism.* San Francisco: Harper and Row, 1986.

Wright, G. Ernest. *The God Who Acts.* Chicago: H. Regnery, 1952.

SCRIPTURE INDEX

153

GENERAL INDEX

235.4
W284 160
9/681

3 4711 00091 8989